External Review for Promotion and Tenure

SPEC Kits

Supporting Effective Library Management for Over Thirty Years

Committed to assisting research and academic libraries in the continuous improvement of management systems, ARL has worked since 1970 to gather and disseminate the best practices for library needs. As part of its committment, ARL maintains an active publications program best known for its SPEC Kits. Through the Collaborative Research/Writing Program, librarians work with ARL staff to design SPEC surveys and write publications. Originally established as an information source for ARL member libraries, the SPEC series has grown to serve the needs of the library community worldwide.

What are SPEC Kits?

Published six times per year, SPEC Kits contain the most valuable, up-to-date information on the latest issues of concern to libraries and librarians today. They are the result of a systematic survey of ARL member libraries on a particular topic related to current practice in the field. Each SPEC Kit contains an executive summary of the survey results; survey questions with tallies and selected comments; the best representative documents from survey participants, such as policies, procedures, handbooks, guidelines, Web sites, records, brochures, and statements; and a selected reading list—both print and online sources—containing the most current literature available on the topic for further study.

Subscribe to SPEC Kits

Subscribers tell us that the information contained in SPEC Kits is valuable to a variety of users, both inside and outside the library. SPEC Kit purchasers use the documentation found in SPEC Kits as a point of departure for research and problem solving because they lend immediate authority to proposals and set standards for designing programs or writing procedure statements. SPEC Kits also function as an important reference tool for library administrators, staff, students, and professionals in allied disciplines who may not have access to this kind of information.

SPEC Kits can be ordered directly from the ARL Publications Distribution Center. To order, call **(301) 362-8196**, fax **(301) 206-9789**, e-mail **pubs@arl.org**, or go to **http://www.arl.org/pubscat/**.

Information on SPEC Kits and the SPEC survey program can be found at **http://www.arl.org/spec/**. The executive summary for each kit after December 1993 can be accessed free of charge at **http://www. arl.org/spec/complete.html**.

SPEC Kit 293

External Review for Promotion and Tenure

August 2006

Tracy Bicknell-Holmes

Chair, Research and Instruction Services

University of Nebraska-Lincoln

Kay Logan-Peters

Chair, Access and Branch Services

University of Nebraska-Lincoln

ASSOCIATION OF RESEARCH LIBRARIES

Series Editor: Lee Anne George

SPEC Kits are published by the

Association of Research Libraries
21 Dupont Circle, NW, Suite 800
Washington, DC 20036-1118
P (202) 296-2296 F (202) 872-0884
http://www.arl.org/spec/
pubs@arl.org

ISSN 0160 3582

ISBN 1-59407-709-6

SPEC Kit 293

External Review for Promotion and Tenure

August 2006

SURVEY RESULTS

REPRESENTATIVE DOCUMENTS

Instructions to External Reviewers

SELECTED RESOURCES

SURVEY RESULTS

EXECUTIVE SUMMARY

Introduction

According to data collected in 2000, librarians at 41 of the 111 reporting academic ARL member libraries (37%) are in tenure track positions; librarians are eligible for a comparable continuing appointment at another 23 academic libraries (21%). In addition, data collected as part of the ARL annual salary survey shows that all but eight academic libraries have a multi-tier ranking system for librarians. This is a clear indication that there is an evaluation process in place for librarian promotion and tenure or other continuing appointment at most ARL libraries.

When a librarian becomes eligible for promotion to the next rank or for permanent appointment many institutions require external reviews of the candidate by peers at other institutions. These reviews become an important part of the evaluation of a librarian's potential for ongoing contributions to the position and the profession.

A literature search reveals that little has been written about the external review process for librarians seeking promotion or continuing appointment. Bradigan and Mularski (1996) conducted a study of criteria used by library administrators to evaluate candidate publications for promotion and tenure and discovered that solicited external assessments were key to their evaluations. Leyson and Black (1998) surveyed Carnegie research institutions on whether they required peer review of faculty. Their study focused primarily on peer review within an institution and mentioned that review by external peers was an important part of the review. Expanding the search to higher education literature, a few additional articles rise to the surface that specifically address external review procedures used to evaluate English (Poston, 1984), nursing school (Reilly, Carlisle, Mikan and Goldsmith, 1996), political science (Schlozman, 1998), and accounting faculty (Schwartz and Schroeder, 1997). Although these articles provide some information that may be applicable to external review of library faculty, nothing in library literature specifically addresses procedures used in academic libraries to conduct external reviews of candidates for promotion and tenure.

The authors of this survey have performed a number of external reviews and have experienced a wide variety of procedures and policies from the requesting libraries. For example, the contents of candidates' portfolios have varied greatly. Some have contained only publications. Others have included a wide variety of material demonstrating work in service and job performance. One included the performance evaluations of the candidate. Some portfolios included the institutions' standards; others did not. The instructions to the reviewers have also varied. Some institutions instructed the reviewer to evaluate the quality of the candidate's work based on the included standards. Some asked the reviewer to evaluate the candidate based on the reviewer's institutional standards. Others asked whether the candidate would receive tenure at the reviewer's institution. Occasionally, the reviewers were offered compensation in exchange for the review.

This survey was designed to identify the policies and procedures that ARL member libraries are using in the external review process for candidates who are eligible for promotion, tenure, or continuing appointment. It examines how external reviewers are identified and asked to participate in the review process, what instructions are given to reviewers, what materials are included in candidates' portfolios, and the criteria for evaluating candidates' portfolios, among other questions.

Background

The survey was distributed to the 123 ARL member libraries in February 2006. Seventy-seven libraries (63%) responded to the survey. Librarians at 35 of the responding institutions have faculty status. Forty-four institutions offer tenure or other permanent appointments (32 with faculty status and 12 without). Slightly more than half of the respondents (39 or 51%) do not require external reviews for librarians who are candidates for promotion, tenure, or continuing appointment. While the majority of these have neither faculty status nor permanent appointments (27 or 69%), they also include six whose librarians have faculty status and 11 that offer tenure or other permanent appointments (five with faculty status and six without).

Of the 38 respondents that do require external reviews, 36 require them for candidates seeking promotion to the next level, 27 require them for tenure candidates, and seven require them for continuous appointment candidates. Not surprisingly, most of these respondents have faculty status and/or offer tenure or other permanent appointment. Librarians at 29 institutions have faculty status and 28 of these require external reviews for promotion candidates. Twenty-seven of these also offer tenure and all require external reviews for tenure candi-

dates. Eight of the nine institutions where librarians do not have faculty status require external reviews for promotion candidates. Six of the nine offer permanent appointments and five of them require external reviews for those candidates.

Review of Terminology

Thirty of the responding institutions that require external review (79%) provided promotion and tenure criteria and procedural documents. Findings from a review of this documentation are included here and in the survey data analysis that follows. A large majority of the procedural documents distinguish reviewers outside an institution from those within the institution with terminology such as "external reviewer," "outside referee," and "external referee" and call their reviews "external evaluations," "outside review letters," or "letters of evaluation." A third specifically contrast these external letters from "solicited letters of support"—letters solicited by the candidate—and internal documents or letters written by supervisors or co-authors/collaborators of the candidate. A few use "references," "referees," "external reviewers," and "evaluation letters" interchangeably and solicit reviews both from writers familiar with the candidate or internal to the university and external writers unfamiliar with or unknown to the candidate. Others refer to "letters of reference" or "references" when discussing procedures that clearly describe external reviews.

Purpose of External Reviews

A few documents include a clear statement of the purpose of external reviews, such as to provide an "independent, unbiased evaluation of the candidate's scholarly attainment." One document states that, "The function of outside reviewers is to provide independent assessments of the candidate's work and professional standing."

In some cases, the purpose of the review can be gleaned from the instructions to the external reviewers—to "provide evaluative information," "evaluative comments," "objective appraisal," "candid appraisal," "critical evaluation," "letter of assessment," "substantive and rigorous evaluation," or "comment in a discriminating and objective way"—or from the criteria for selecting external reviewers, such as "Objective evaluators without conflicts of interest," and "unbiased, external evaluators." Based on these statements, for nearly half of the institutions external reviews are to be unbiased evaluations or critical assessments of the candidates.

At three institutions, the language in the instructions to the external reviewers or from the criteria for selecting external reviewers reveals that the purpose of the external review is to put the candidate in a positive light. For example: "Your name has been suggested…as someone who could write a recommendation on [candidate's] behalf;" referees contacted by the candidate who have "agreed to write positive written letters of recommendation;" and external reviewers are "expected to display the academic professional and his/her activities and achievements in the most advantageous light." At one of these institutions, the positive letters are paired with letters designed to evaluate the candidate critically and objectively.

Five institutions (17%) require external reviews only for those candidates seeking the top one or two highest ranks and this occurs primarily in systems with four or five ranks. One institution requires external reviews only for candidates seeking continuing appointment.

Soliciting Reviews

At 30 of the responding libraries (79%), candidates for promotion or tenure identify potential external reviewers. In all but six of these libraries, they receive assistance from review committees and/or the library director. It is also not unusual for supervisors to assist candidates in this process. Personnel officers are involved at only three of the libraries. At five of the eight libraries where the candidate does not identify reviewers, the com-

mittee and/or library director most often does so. At one library, the external reviewers are those library directors who serve on the visiting Library Advisory Council. At another, the candidate's supervisor identifies reviewers, while at the third it is the unit director, who may not be the candidate's immediate supervisor.

Somewhat unexpectedly, the documentation of five institutions specifies that the candidate has the opportunity to identify people (s)he would prefer not be asked to provide an external review and why. At two of these institutions, a person who has been identified by the candidate as inappropriate may still be asked to write a review, but the review must be accompanied by the candidate's objection and a rationale on why (s)he was chosen as a reviewer against the candidate's expressed concerns.

Nearly three-fourths of the respondents indicated that reviewers are selected based on their reputation in the candidate's area of expertise. For six, this is the only criterion, the remainder chose multiple criteria. Rank of the reviewer is the second most important factor and some select reviewers because their home institution has similar promotion and tenure criteria. Other criteria include the reviewer's knowledge of the candidate's contributions and the favorable reputation of the reviewer's institution. For example, six institutions specifically require that reviewers come from a "comparable," "peer," or "benchmark" institution or otherwise comment on the quality of the institution where the reviewer works. Four require that reviewers be considered experts in their field. Five require a specific rank for the external reviewer, most commonly at the rank to which the candidate aspires or above. In one case, only full professors or the equivalent can be selected as external reviewers.

Some libraries seek input from reviewers who have had limited or no contact with the candidate while others seek out reviewers with knowledge of the candidate and his/her contributions. According to a review of the procedural documents, five institutions either require that letters come both from reviewers familiar with the candidate and those who are not, or allow a portion of the reviewers to be familiar with the candidate. Three specifically exclude co-authors, people in direct supervisory line, and former students or teachers from writing reviews. One of these states that reviewers must be "sufficiently at arms length" to provide an objective assessment. Another six state that reviewers should be knowledgeable about the candidate or the candidate's accomplishments, or should be people who have direct knowledge about the candidate's performance. Interestingly, one of these institutions also specifically instructs the reviewer to supply an "objective appraisal."

On average, institutions seek five reviewers for each candidate. The minimum number of external reviews sought was one; three respondents solicit up to 10. According to the documentation, three institutions require an increasing number of external reviews with increasing rank. Forty percent do not specify a number of external reviewers required while a third state a minimum number of reviewers required. According to the survey responses, five of the ten institutions that specify a minimum number regularly require more than the minimum when soliciting reviews while two typically request the minimum number required by their institutions.

Many survey respondents convene a review committee to oversee promotion and tenure activities. These committees, or the committee chair, most frequently make the initial contact with potential reviewers (14 responses or 38%). Library directors and personnel officers are next most likely to initiate contact. At only four libraries do immediate supervisors contact reviewers. In no case does the candidate contact the reviewer directly.

Very rarely are reviewers unable to participate. Seven libraries (19%) indicated that a request to serve as a reviewer had never been rejected. Occasionally, a reviewer is unable to provide input due to other work commitments or because they are deemed ineligible due to rank, lack of tenure,

etc. In some cases, reviewers simply do not respond to letters seeking input on a candidate's portfolio. Although the numbers are small and probably not large enough to illustrate a clear pattern, there does not seem to be any correlation between the way an external review is solicited and the likelihood that the request will be turned down.

The Candidate's Portfolio

Few candidates have complete control of the contents of the portfolio sent to reviewers. Most often the contents are dictated by administrative/procedural requirements (17 responses or 46%). Occasionally, candidates are able to select materials to include in their portfolios, in combination with required materials (11 or 30%).

Generally, the candidate's portfolio is sent after initial contact has been made with a potential reviewer and the person has agreed to serve (24 responses or 67%). Materials included in the portfolio nearly always include the candidate's curriculum vitae (CV) or "factual résumé" (33 or 89%) and evidence of publishing or scholarly activities (26 or 70%). Respondents who send the CV/résumé with the candidate's portfolio tend to send additional supporting documentation, as well. A significant number include a summary of accomplishments written by the candidate (20 or 54%), evidence of creative and service activities (17 or 46% each), and job related materials (13 or 35%). Other materials include criteria for assessment, institutional documents, peer assessments of teaching, and letters of reference. One institution reported that they sent "whatever the candidate submits." According to the procedural documents reviewed, only one institution sends copies of performance appraisals with the candidate's portfolio.

A third of the respondents (12) send the reviewer a candidate's portfolio along with the initial letter of inquiry. The procedural documents of five of these institutions include a list of the portfolio contents. All of these institutions submit the candidate's CV or résumé. Other documents include the institution's criteria/standards for promotion and tenure, copies of the candidate's publications, the candidate's statement of accomplishments, research, etc., and the candidate's position description, among others.

Four respondents do not send external reviewers either the CV or résumé. A review of these institutions' documentation reveals that the reviewers are asked to comment only on firsthand knowledge of the candidate or are required/expected to be familiar with at least some aspect of the candidate's work. Of these four institutions, two send a candidate's summary statement of accomplishments, one sends publications, and one sends nothing from the candidate's portfolio.

Instructions to Reviewers

The majority of respondents (30 or 81%) indicate that external reviewers are asked to evaluate the candidate based on the promotion and tenure standards of the candidate's library. All but one send the standards or a URL where they may be retrieved with the candidate's portfolio; the other sends the university's minimum guidelines for promotion and tenure reviews. Three institutions (8%) ask the reviewer to evaluate the candidate using the criteria of the reviewer's library. Interestingly, two of these also send copies of the criteria of the candidate's library with the portfolio.

One institution responded that they do not specify criteria with which to evaluate a candidate; three had other criteria. A review of the documentation for these four institutions shows that they ask reviewers to comment only on aspects of the candidate's work with which the reviewer is familiar, have firsthand knowledge or have directly observed, or instruct them to comment on both the evidence in the folder and their personal knowledge about the candidate.

Reviewers are asked to evaluate a variety of the candidate's activities and areas of performance. The candidate's record of publishing or scholarly activities is the most common area evaluated by external reviewers (34 or 89%). The candidate's creative and service activities tie for second with 25 responses each (66%). Job performance is included in the evaluation by about a third of respondents. According to the documents reviewed, the most common areas reviewers were asked to evaluate include pattern of productivity, quality and significance of the candidate's work, the impact of the candidate's work on the institution and/or the profession, and the potential for further growth and/or continued professional productivity.

A reading of the procedural documents shows that three of the institutions ask reviewers to make a recommendation on whether the candidate should be awarded promotion or continuing appointment, while an equal number specifically tell reviewers not to make a recommendation on whether the candidate should be awarded promotion or continuing appointment. Ten institutions ask external reviewers to compare the candidate to librarians at other institutions or in similar positions. Eight ask that external reviewers evaluate or estimate the candidate's stature or standing in the field, or comment on the degree of recognition the candidate has achieved in the profession. For example, one library asks reviewers to compare the candidate with others in positions nationally and internationally, another requests that reviewers evaluate the recognition the candidate has received at regional, national and international levels, and a third asks that reviewers evaluate the state/regional/national/international stature of the candidate as a result of his/her work. One institution asks the evaluator to comment on the manner in which the candidate's work "enhances the effectiveness or standing" of the university.

Reviewers are asked to comment on other aspects of the candidate's performance, as well. External reviewers for one library are asked "whether [the candidate] would be ranked among the most capable and promising librarians in his/her area;" another asks reviewers to evaluate the originality of the candidate's achievements; yet another requests that reviewers evaluate the independence of the candidate's contributions.

Fifty-four percent of the respondents (20) give the reviewer more than one month to complete the review while 46% (17) allow two weeks to one month for completion of the review. No respondent gives the reviewer less than two weeks. If the reviewer has questions about the review process or instructions, in almost every case (s)he is instructed to contact the person who made the initial contact. In one case, the personnel officer makes first contact, but the reviewer is told to contact the library director if there are questions. In another case, just the opposite is true. In a third case, the review committee makes the initial contact, but the library director is the contact for questions. The candidate is never designated as a contact.

Relationship of the Portfolio Contents to Reviewer Instructions

A comparison of the responses to the questions about what the reviewer is asked to evaluate and what documentation is submitted as part of the candidate's portfolio reveals that the majority of respondents (28 or 76%) provide sufficient evidence of the candidate's performance in each area they ask the external reviewer to evaluate. A few send very little material, but also only ask for a limited review. For example, one respondent only sends examples of the candidate's publications and only asks the reviewer to evaluate those publications. Another sends only a summary statement, but instructs the reviewer to "evaluate only areas within the criteria of which the reviewer has personal knowledge." A third doesn't send a portfolio at all, but explains that the "reviewer is asked to comment on specific accomplishments and/or position responsibilities suggested by the candidate."

What is notable is the number of respondents who rely heavily on the candidate's CV or summary statement for evidence of performance. For example, three respondents send only a CV or summary, four send both a CV and summary, and two

send a CV and publications. All ask the reviewer to evaluate publications, creative and service activities, and job performance. Also of note are the practices of the three institutions that stated the purpose of the review is to show the candidate in a positive light. One of these sends the reviewers the CV and publications; the other two send all categories of portfolio materials. Together these examples raise the unanswered question of what is sufficient evidence of the quality of the performance the reviewer is being asked to evaluate.

Procedural documents were available for seven of the institutions that ask reviewers to evaluate a candidate's job performance. In two cases, reviewers are specifically chosen because they are acquainted with the candidate's work or have a professional connection with him/her. In two others, reviewers include both those who are familiar with the candidate and those who are not. The remaining three documents were unclear on these points.

Estimated Costs of Time Spent on a Review

Not surprisingly, none of the survey respondents track or have tried to track the costs of requiring external reviews for candidates. None track or try to estimate the time spent by candidates and others in preparing documentation for external reviews, either. Likewise, none of the respondents compensate reviewers financially for conducting reviews of their candidates.

In the absence of this information, the survey authors developed a rough estimate of the cost of conducting external reviews using data available from this survey and the ARL annual salary survey. Administrative and department chair positions and library faculty with longer years of service are most likely to be external reviewers. Using salary survey data on the average salaries for these positions and assuming a 40-hour workweek for a 52-week year, an average hourly rate of each position was calculated. According to this survey's respondents, one review takes 5.9 hours of labor, on average, and 24 hours at most. The cost of conducting one review was calculated by multiplying the hourly rate by the mean and maximum amount of time reported for conducting a review. The table of data that was generated is below.

A director completing one review a year in 5.9 hours would cost $479, while a director taking the maximum number of hours for one review would cost $1,948. At the other end of the scale, the cost of a cataloging or reference librarian conducting one external review might range from $163 to $682. Clearly the cost of conducting external reviews varies considerably based on the position level of the reviewer, the amount of time (s)he spends, and the number of reviews conducted each year.

The Role of External Reviews in the Promotion and Tenure Process

External reviews of candidates appear to carry fairly significant weight with both peers and administrators. Seventy-nine percent of respondents (27) rated the influence of external review letters on administrators as a four or five on a five-point scale where five equaled "very much;" only one rated the influence below a three. The influence of external review letters on peers was slightly lower; 66% of respondents (23) rated their influence as a four or five, the remaining 34% (12) as a three.

Responding to Review Requests

Seventy-two percent of the survey respondents (53) said that librarians at their institutions conduct reviews of candidates at other institutions. Of the 38 institutions that require external reviews of their candidates, only one institution said they do not conduct external reviews of candidates from other institutions. Of the institutions that do not require external reviews of their candidates, 46% (18) accept invitations to review candidates from other institutions.

Estimates of the number of external reviews by library faculty and time spent on them are anecdotal or rough estimates at best, as this work is often not reported to their home institutions. However, survey respondents estimated that the number of reviews conducted annually ranged from one to 22. The average was 6.6. Reviewers spent a minimum of 30 minutes and a maximum of 24 hours on each review or an average of 5.9 hours.

Privacy Concerns

One concern about external reviews that came out in the comments and in the review of procedural documents is the confidentiality of external review letters. Often, a candidate's right to see an external review of his/her candidacy is dictated by state

Position	Average Salary**	Hourly Rate***	Cost Estimate to Conduct One Review	
			Mean (5.9 hrs)	Maximum (24 hrs)
Director	$168,894	$81.20	$479.07	$1,948.78
Associate Director	$102,484	$49.27	$290.70	$1,182.51
Assistant Director	$92,478	$44.46	$262.32	$1,067.05
Head, Branch	$70,179	$33.74	$199.07	$809.76
Department Chair*	$67,490	$32.45	$191.44	$778.73
Reference				
over 14 years experience	$59,134	$28.43	$167.74	$682.32
Cataloging				
over 14 years experience	$57,631	$27.71	$163.47	$664.97
* calculated as an average of all types of department heads				
** Source: "Table 25: Average Salaries of ARL University Librarians by Position and Geographic Region," *ARL Annual Salary Survey 2005–06*, Washington, DC: Association of Research Libraries, 2005.				
*** Average salary / 2080 hours				

law or university policy. More than a third of the documents reviewed required that external review letters remain strictly confidential; the candidate is not allowed to see them or respond to their contents. A small number state that the candidate can request to see the letter in redacted form where all identifying information is blacked out. In one case, the candidate has five days to respond to the contents of a letter, but it is not clear whether the letter is in redacted form. In another case, state law dictates that the candidate has the right to see external review letters if (s)he makes a request. It is not clear whether the letters are in redacted form or identifying information is available to the candidate who reviews them. In two cases, the institution allows the candidate to choose among options: waiving their rights to see the letter, seeing the letter in redacted form, or seeing the complete letter with identification of the reviewer included. In both cases, the reviewer is apprised of whether the candidate will see the letter when they conduct the review.

Unique Features of the Review Process

The review of procedural documents also revealed these interesting features of the external review process:

- A small number of institutions specifically state that external review letters may be used again for another review at a later date. For example, documentation from one university says that external review letters "may be used again" but cannot be used selectively. All of the letters must be used or none of them may be.
- The documentation for another university talks about "interviews with referees," but it isn't clear whether this is done in addition to a written external evaluation or in lieu of a written review.
- In one document, knowledge of the candidate is considered "evidence of the candidate's

visibility" and is defined as having heard the candidate present a paper, having read an article by the candidate, etc.
- At another university, the library faculty personnel committee reads the external review letters and prepares a "written analysis of the validity and significance of the reviews received."
- Three institutions specifically require that all letters solicited must be included in the file whether negative or positive.
- Several institutions also state that negative input from external evaluators should be addressed rather than ignored.
- Nearly all of the institutions that supplied procedural documents specifically require reviewers or the person who selects the reviewer to document the relationship of the reviewer to the candidate.
- Two institutions specifically require that letters written to solicit outside evaluation contain neutral language about the candidate.

Conclusion

These survey results clearly show that external reviews carry weight in tenure and promotion decisions with both peers and administrators. They also show a significant amount of collegiality on the part of faculty who are asked to perform external reviews. Although there are some similarities and patterns in the process of conducting outside peer reviews, procedures vary across institutions. In some cases, these variations are due to institutional policy. In others, they seem to be choices made by the library faculty in developing their internal procedures.

Nonetheless, what is striking about these survey results is how closely they mirror other studies of the external review process in some areas, yet differ widely in others. For example, when Reilly, Carlisle, Mikan, and Goldsmith surveyed nursing schools, they found that external reviews were required by 60% of institutions for tenure and 64%

for promotion, compared with this survey's results of 31% and 43% respectively. (1996, p. 370)

Schlozman researched the external review process of political science faculty from the point of view of full professors who completed the reviews. She found that faculty spent an average of 10.6 hours on reviews of candidates for tenure and nine hours on candidates for promotion, compared to the estimate of 5.9 hours in this survey. (1998, p. 624) It would be interesting to survey library faculty directly to see if the estimates from those who have completed external reviews are closer to those estimated by the political science faculty. Schlozman also found that the burden of completing external reviews was shared very unevenly in her profession. This may be true in academic libraries, too, since at eleven of the responding institutions reviewers complete fewer than five evaluations a year while at three they complete more than ten.

None of the literature found on external reviews discussed cost estimates for the process and no one

requiring external reviews in this survey is tracking the cost, either. The estimate of the cost of an external review is very rough and only takes into account the time spent by the faculty performing the reviews. Perhaps the dollar cost of the process is not as critical as ensuring that good decisions on promotion and tenure are being made, though. As one survey respondent noted, "Money spent on getting a tenure decision correct is money very well spent."

This survey begins to describe the external review process in research libraries and points to areas where more research could be undertaken. Additional research could attempt to more accurately estimate the costs of personnel and resources for portfolio preparation, identify best practices, and answer questions such as: What is the success rate for candidates who undergo external review? How does the success rate relate to the rigorousness of the process? What are the privacy issues? Do all promotions require external review or only those to specific ranks?

SURVEY QUESTIONS and RESPONSES

The SPEC survey on External Review for Promotion and Tenure was designed by Tracy Bicknell-Holmes, Chair, Research and Instructional Services, and Kay Logan-Peters, Chair, Access and Branch Services, at the University of Nebraska-Lincoln. These results are based on data submitted by 77 of the 123 ARL member libraries (63%) by the deadline of March 15, 2006. The survey's introductory text and questions are reproduced below, followed by the response data and selected comments from the respondents.

According to data collected in 2000, librarians at 41 of the 111 reporting academic ARL member libraries (37%) are in tenure track positions; librarians are eligible for a comparable continuing appointment at another 23 academic libraries (21%). In addition, data collected as part of the ARL annual salary survey shows that all but eight academic libraries have a multi-tier ranking system for librarians. This is a clear indication that there is an evaluation process in place for librarian promotion and tenure or other continuing appointment at most ARL libraries. When a librarian becomes eligible for promotion to the next rank or for permanent appointment, some institutions require external reviews of the candidate by peers at another institution. These reviews become an important part of the evaluation of a librarian's potential for ongoing contributions to the position and the profession.

A quick literature search reveals that little has been written about the external review process for librarians. The authors of this survey have performed a number of external reviews and have experienced a wide variety of procedures and policies from the requesting libraries. For example, the contents of candidates' portfolios have varied greatly. Some have contained only publications. Others have included a wide variety of material demonstrating work in service and job performance. One included the performance evaluations of the candidate. Some portfolios included the institutions' standards; others did not. The instructions to the reviewers have also varied. Some institutions instructed the reviewer to evaluate the quality of the candidate's work based on the included standards. Some asked the reviewer to evaluate the candidate based on the reviewer's institutional standards. Others asked whether the candidate would receive tenure at the reviewer's institution. Occasionally, the reviewers were offered compensation in exchange for the review.

This survey is designed to identify the policies and procedures that ARL member libraries are using in the external review process for candidates who are eligible for promotion, tenure, or continuing appointment. It examines how external reviewers are identified and asked to participate in the review process; what instructions are given to reviewers; what materials are included in candidates' portfolios; and the criteria for evaluating candidates' portfolios, among other questions.

BACKGROUND

1. Does your library require external reviews of librarians who are candidates for promotion, tenure, or continuing appointment (P/T/CA)? N=77

Yes, for promotion	36	47%
Yes, for tenure	27	35%
Yes, for continuing appointment	7	9%

Yes Total	38	49%	
No	39	51%	Please skip to question 18.

If yes, in what year did your library begin requiring external reviews of P/T/CA candidates? N=24

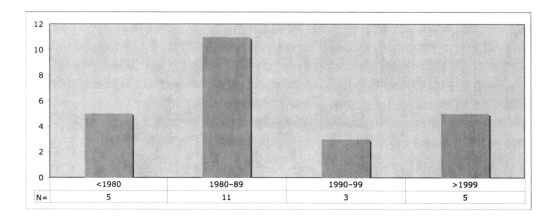

N=	<1980	1980–89	1990–99	>1999
	5	11	3	5

SOLICITING REVIEWS

2. At your library, who identifies potential external reviewers? Please check all that apply. N=38

The candidate	30	79%
Library dean/director	16	42%
Review committee or review committee chair	13	34%
The candidate's immediate supervisor	10	26%
Personnel officer	4	11%
Other, please explain	6	16%

Selected Comments from Respondents

"Two are nominated by candidate, three by library (Dean with advice of EC)."

"Candidates identify three possible reviewers and the Personnel Officer selects one of the three."

"Final recommendation is made by Unit Director, but others are consulted in the process."

"The candidate's associate dean."

"The external reviewers are those library directors who serve on the (visiting) Library Advisory Council."

"Unit director who may or may not be the immediate supervisor."

3. **What criteria are used to identify potential external reviewers? Please check all that apply. N=38**

The reviewer's reputation in the candidate's field of expertise	28	74%
The rank of the reviewer (assistant, associate, professor/librarian)	20	53%
The reviewer's library's promotion and tenure standards	14	37%
Other, please explain	16	42%

Selected Comments from Respondents

"Appropriateness of reviewer's position relative to the candidate's position"

"None"

"Other criteria include the reviewer's professional relationship to the candidate and the reviewer's ability to evaluate the candidate's work."

"Relative standing of institution, prefer faculty, must not be a research collaborator of candidate"

"Reputation of reviewer's institution"

"Reviewer's knowledge of candidate's contributions"

"Reviewer's knowledge of the candidate's activities, accomplishments, contributions to library and profession"

"Reviewer's knowledge of the candidate's work and professional activities"

"Subject area"

"The external reviewers are those library directors who serve on the (visiting) Library Advisory Council."

"The reviewer's academic institution"

"The reviewer's knowledge of the candidate's achievements during the period under review"

"The reviewer's publication record, activity in professional associations, experience with faculty status, and employment at one of our peer institutions."

"We look for a reviewer from a comparable institution, reviewer holds a position at a comparable institution that allows him/her to serve as a reviewer and, if possible, the reviewer comes from an institution that has a similar personnel process/system."

"What part of the candidate's qualifications the individual can address."

4. **How many external reviewers are sought for each P/T/CA candidate? N=37**

Minimum	Maximum	Mean	Median	Std Dev
1	10	5.3	5.0	2.2

5. **Who contacts potential external reviewers? N=38**

Review committee or review committee chair	14	38%
Library dean/director	8	22%
Personnel officer	8	22%
The candidate's immediate supervisor	4	11%
The candidate	0	0%
Other, please explain	4	8%

Selected Comments from Respondents

"Candidate's immediate supervisor OR personnel officer."

"This is a shared responsibility between the Personnel Officer and the Promotion and Tenure Committee Chair."

"Assistant to the Dean on behalf of the Dean."

"Unit director."

6. In your experience, how often are potential reviewers unable or unwilling to perform an external review? N=37

Frequently	1	3%
Occasionally	29	78%
Never	7	19%

Selected Comments from Respondents

"'Rarely' would be a better answer. Very few say no."

"Almost never. They are asked to nominate alternates."

"Frequently is about 1 out of 3."

"Only if overextended due to other requests or personal reasons."

"Sometimes a reviewer will not respond. Many supervisors write to six or more reviewers to ensure that we get at least three letters. We also suggest the supervisor provide at least a month for the reviewer to write and respond."

"The one or two times that the reviewer was not able to participate resulted from their unavailability during the review period."

"This occurs when the reviewer discloses information that makes the reviewer ineligible; such as not having faculty rank, or not tenured."

THE CANDIDATE'S PORTFOLIO

7. When is the candidate's portfolio sent to the external reviewer? N=36

After (s)he has agreed to perform the review	24	67%
With initial inquiry letter	12	33%

8. What materials typically go into the portfolio that is sent to the external reviewer? Check all that apply. N=37

Curriculum Vitae	33	89%
Evidence of publishing or scholarly activities	26	70%
Summary of accomplishments	20	54%
Evidence of creative activities	17	46%
Evidence of service activities	17	46%
Job related materials	13	35%
Other, please explain	11	30%

Selected Comments from Respondents

"Candidate's narrative statement."

"Candidate's statement, promotion & tenure document."

"Criteria for assessment."

"Criteria for promotion and/or continuing appointment; position description."

"CV, accomplishments, job-related materials may be sent; not required."

"Peer assessments of teaching, self-assessment of progress, evidence of professional practice, evidence of teaching, etc."

"Library's statement on promotion and tenure. In past years, also include candidate's statement of research goals and accomplishments."

"Performance appraisals, letters of reference."

"Statement of research interests & service statement & our criteria document."

"The actual application and the criteria and weightings that we use."

"The portfolio is not sent to external reviewer. Reviewer is asked to comment on specific accomplishments and or position responsibilities suggested by the candidate."

"Whatever the candidate submits."

9. What level of input does the candidate have over the contents of the portfolio? N=37

Administration and/or procedures dictate the contents of the portfolios	17	46%
Some documents are required, the candidate decides on other		
documentation to include	11	30%
The candidate decides what to send	3	8%
Other, please explain	6	16%

Selected Comments from Respondents

"Usually the supervisor just sends a letter; in some cases a CV or summary of recent activities is included."

"The candidate communicates to the promotion committee which accomplishments and or position responsibilities each external reviewer should be asked to comment on."

"Candidate provides CV and publications (max 3)."

"Supervisor determines with suggestions from candidate."

"Procedures require CV & criteria and accomplishments; candidate decides on other documents."

"The second option is the closest. Standards indicate specific documentation that is required; the candidates can put in other evidence in the case file. The case file is sent to the reviewers."

INSTRUCTIONS TO REVIEWERS

10. By what criteria or standards are reviewers asked to evaluate the candidate? N=37

By our (the requesting) library's P/T/CA criteria	30	81%
By reviewer's library's P/T/CA criteria	3	8%
No specific criteria recommended	1	3%
Other, please explain	3	8%

Selected Comments from Respondents

"Reviewer's knowledge of the candidate's contribution."

"Significance and impact of scholarly activity."

"By the standards of leading higher education institutions."

"[By our criteria], also by our institution's criteria."

If by your (the requesting) library's P/T/CA criteria, is a copy of the criteria sent to the reviewer? N=30

Yes	29	96%
No	1	4%

Selected Comments from Respondents

"The reviewer is given the URL for locating the document which outlines the criteria for the institution."

"Send a cover letter and the university's minimum guidelines for P&T reviews."

"We also send [the university's] criteria for P&T."

11. Please indicate which aspects of the candidate's performance reviewers are asked to evaluate. Check all that apply. N=38

Record of publishing or scholarly activities	34	89%
Record of creative activities	25	66%
Record of service activities	25	66%
Job performance	13	34%
Other, please explain	12	32%

Selected Comments from Respondents

"'Professional accomplishments and activities'—specifically how the candidate 'enhances the effectiveness and standing of the Libraries, demonstrates his/her ability to meet the responsibilities of the desired rank, and enhances and contributes to the profession.'"

"All of the above (we have four criteria—job performance, professional activities, university and community service, research and creative activity."

"Any and all areas with which the reviewer is familiar (from among: job performance, professional contribution, and service.)"

"Career development, contributions to the discipline, national reputation."

"Involvement at the national level whether or not it constitutes service."

"It depends; some are asked to address scholarly activities; others service, etc."

"Local and national/international committees, leadership."

"Only areas within criteria of which the reviewer has personal knowledge."

"Other knowledge they may have."

"Primarily research and scholarly work (Section 5.2) of the standards—Section 5 is Practice of Professional Skills."

"Some or all of the above, depending on the relationship and professional expertise of the external reviewer to the candidate."

"Tenurability or promotability comparable to their institution."

12. How long are external reviewers given to complete the review? N=37

More than one month	20	54%
Two weeks to one month	17	46%
Less than two weeks	0	0%

13. Who are reviewers instructed to contact if they have questions about the review process or instructions? N=38

Review committee or review committee chair	12	32%
Library dean/director	10	26%
Personnel officer	8	21%
The candidate's immediate supervisor	5	13%
The candidate	0	0%
Other, please explain	3	8%

Selected Comments from Respondents

"This is shared between the personnel officer and the committee chair."

"Either committee chair or personnel officer."

"The unit director."

ESTIMATED COSTS

14. Does your library track or try to estimate the cost of external reviews in terms of administrative and staff time, costs of copying and postage, etc.? N=38

Yes	0	0%
No	38	100%

"As external reviews are required by the Standards (university and ours), we have not invested the time to determine the costs."

"Money spent on getting a tenure decision correct is money very well spent!"

15. Does your library track or try to estimate how much time candidates spend preparing documentation for an external reviewer? N=37

Yes	0	0%
No	37	100%

16. Does your library compensate external reviewers? N=37

Yes	0	0%
No	37	100%

"We thank them as much and as sincerely as we can!!"

17. On a scale of 1 to 5, where 1 equals very little and 5 equals very much, how much influence does the evaluation of a candidate by an external reviewer carry during the P/T/CA process? N=35

	N	1	2	3	4	5
Influences the candidate's peer evaluators	35	—	—	12	15	8
Influences the institution's administrators	34	—	1	6	15	12

RESPONDING TO REVIEW REQUESTS

18. Do librarians at your institution complete external reviews of candidates for promotion, tenure, or continuing appointment at other institutions? N=74

Yes	53	72%
No	21	28%

If yes, about how many external reviews are conducted by librarians at your institution annually? N=21

Minimum	Maximum	Mean	Median	Std Dev
1	22	6.6	4.0	6.1

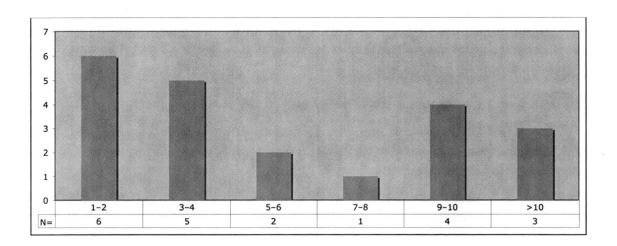

	1–2	3–4	5–6	7–8	9–10	>10
N=	6	5	2	1	4	3

On average, how much time does a librarian spend on each external review for another institution? N=21

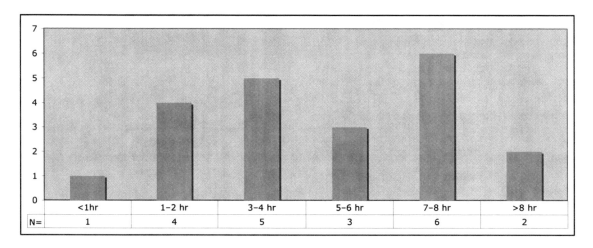

Minimum	Maximum	Mean	Median	Std Dev
.5 hours	24 hours	5.9 hours	5.0 hours	5.0

	<1hr	1–2 hr	3–4 hr	5–6 hr	7–8 hr	>8 hr
N=	1	4	5	3	6	2

ADDITIONAL COMMENTS

19. Please submit any additional information regarding the external review process at your library that may assist the authors in accurately analyzing the results of this survey.

Selected Comments from Respondents

"We have had a dual track system since the early 1990s: Librarian Faculty and Regular (tenure-track/tenured) Faculty. External reviews are required for tenure-track positions and optional for librarian track. We only have one librarian on tenure track at present; we have not tenured any librarian since the late 1990s."

"At our institution continuing appointment and tenure are synonymous."

"The only promotion that bears external review is that of being promoted from Associate Librarian to Full Librarian."

"[Our] librarians achieved faculty status in 1968. We believe that external review was undoubtedly part of the process from the beginning at our institution."

"There is no way we can track how much external reviewing our librarians are doing and how much time it takes. We probably get a modest amount of requests a year (less than a dozen, if that many) and it probably takes people several hours (at least four hours and probably much longer at times) to do an assessment and write an evaluation."

"[We have] five librarian ranks. Outside reviewers are used only in those cases where librarians are being considered for promotion to Librarian IV or V. Our Personnel Program for Librarians is under review and the current way that we use outside reviewers is one area of the program that might very well be changed."

"External reviews should be a critical component of gaining tenure or, in our case, continuing appointment in any research institution. I believe our institution has been derelict in having not required it to date. Not requiring rigorous external evaluations of librarians keeps them in a second-class citizenship in relation to the professorate."

"Librarians are library faculty, which is one of four types of faculty here. We are non tenure-track. For promotion to assistant, associate, or full, librarians can certainly furnish names of external people as reviewers, but we do not require external reviews. Second, when names of externals reviewers are given, we furnish a minimum of information, but which does include the criteria and the candidate's CV."

"Solicitation for comments from librarians at our institution would come directly to the librarian and be considered confidential. Therefore we would have no way of knowing the volume or the level of effort our librarians may be putting into such solicitations."

"Our librarians do not have faculty rank or status. They serve on yearly renewable appointments."

"Our staff is involved in reviewing sporadically, and not frequently. The number I've given occurred within the last five years. Eleven librarians out of 102 took part in at least one review in that time frame. At the top of the range was someone who's done five. I then asked them to gauge the time spent in work days (=7 hrs). Here the range was from 2 hours to 21. I tossed out the person who spent three work days on one review(!) to get the average of four hours."

"Our University Library Director and some AULs do external reviews for individuals at other institutions on occasion."

"Question #4: The number of reviewers depends on the rank to which the candidate seeks promotion. The candidate is the one who recommends the reviewers. Question #7: The library does not send candidate's portfolio to reviewers. Question #18: Library administration does not track who participates from existing library staff in the external review of colleagues at other institutions. It is believed that tracking this type of professional service would violate the confidentiality of the review process and that those persons who are asked for an external review for a person at another institution would decline to reveal this information."

"I am aware that some staff members, particularly at the higher levels, participate in external reviews of staff from other institutions. However, we have no data or further information about numbers of reviews or time used for that purpose."

"Librarians are not faculty; they are academic appointees. Career status is awarded after a suitable trial period. Letters from referees/reviewers are required for promotion in rank and other actions, i.e., acceleration and distinguished status."

"We are strongly considering inclusion of external reviews in our rank and status process."

"We have two librarians that spend about four hours on each external review. One librarian spent 12 hours but it was her first (and only) external review."

"We have an internal peer review process but do not require external reviews."

RESPONDING INSTITUTIONS

University of Alabama

University at Albany, SUNY

University of Alberta

University of Arizona

Arizona State University

Auburn University

Boston College

Brigham Young University

Brown University

University at Buffalo, SUNY

University of California, Davis

University of California, Irvine

University of California, Los Angeles

University of California, San Diego

University of California, Santa Barbara

Canada Institute for Scientific and Technical Information

Case Western Reserve University

University of Chicago

Colorado State University

University of Connecticut

Cornell University

University of Delaware

Duke University

George Washington University

Universityof Georgia

Georgia Institute of Technology

University of Guelph

University of Houston

University of Illinois at Chicago

University of Illinois at Urbana-Champaign

Indiana University Bloomington

University of Iowa

Iowa State University

University of Kansas

Kent State University

University of Kentucky

Library of Congress

Louisiana State University

University of Louisville

University of Manitoba

University of Maryland

University of Massachusetts Amherst

Massachusetts Institute of Technology

University of Miami

University of Michigan

Université de Montréal

University of Nebraska–Lincoln

North Carolina State University

Northwestern University

University of Notre Dame

Ohio University

University of Oklahoma

University of Oregon

University of Pennsylvania

Pennsylvania State University

University of Pittsburgh

Purdue University

Rice University

Rutgers University

University of Saskatchewan

University of Southern California

Southern Illinois University Carbondale

Syracuse University

University of Tennessee

University of Texas at Austin

Texas A&M University

University of Utah

Vanderbilt University

University of Virginia

Virginia Tech

University of Washington

Washington State University

Washington University in St. Louis

University of Western Ontario

University of Wisconsin–Madison

Yale University

REPRESENTATIVE DOCUMENTS

External Review Procedures

SECTION V: LETTERS FROM OUTSIDE EVALUATORS

Note to candidate and to department head: The function of outside evaluators is to provide *independent* assessments of the candidate's work and professional standing. For this reason, it is essential that the candidate not influence, or attempt to influence, the assessment provided by the outside evaluators. The candidate may submit names of possible evaluators to the department head; however, no more than half of the total evaluators may be from the candidate's list.

If the candidate has engaged in extensive collaboration, and the ability of the candidate to make independent contributions may be difficult to ascertain, it may be helpful to request letters from one or more of his/her collaborators describing the extent and nature of the candidate's contribution to the collaboration.

A sample letter to outside evaluators is included as Appendix D. Deviate from the wording of the sample letter only with the permission of your dean. The content of all questions included in the sample letter must be included in your letter unless you have permission from the Provost to eliminate.

Include in the dossier:

☐ **One sample copy of request letter sent by department head or head of department review committee**

☐ **Summary of process used to select outside evaluators to be provided by department head**
  - ☐ List all outside evaluators recommended by candidate
  - ☐ List additional outside evaluators recommended and by whom
  - ☐ List all outside evaluators contacted whether or not they agreed to serve as evaluators
  - ☐ Describe criteria used in selecting outside evaluators
  - ☐ Describe who selected final list of outside evaluators

☐ **Brief statement on each evaluator's national or international standing**
  (Identify those who can be judged as independent of the candidate. **Do not** include full CV.)

☐ **Letters from Outside Evaluators**
  - ☐ Three to eight letters from similar academic departments outside the University of Arizona dated within one year of the department committee's report
  - ☐ All letters must be from *independent*, outside evaluators who are not the candidate's major professor, co-author, dissertation advisor, or otherwise closely associated with candidate
  - ☐ *All* letters received from outside evaluators must be included

☐ **Letters from Collaborators**
  - ☐ Letter(s) describing extent and nature of candidate's contribution to collaboration when candidate has engaged in extensive collaborative work

☐ **Letters of Evaluation**
  Department heads should clarify how letters of evaluation were solicited.
  - ☐ By University of Arizona faculty colleagues
  - ☐ By present or former graduate students

ASU Libraries Home
Find...
Library Services
Research Assistance
About the Libraries
Need Help?
Go to a Specific
Library

ASU Home

My Account
Search this Site

Catalog Quick Search: Keyword ⬍ for [   ] Go

Librarians' Council

G.2.4: Letters of Reference

Effective 8/18/2000

In total, letters of reference should present a well-rounded representation of the academic professional's career. Referees should be chosen carefully as these individuals will be expected to display the academic professional and his/her activities and achievements in the most advantageous light. Letters that are less strong, "damn with faint praise" or never arrive, may weaken the academic professional's packet rather than promote it. When selecting references, consider the following guidelines.

1. Contact the referee beforehand to confirm that he/she is willing to write a letter of reference and that he/she will be available during the critical period.

2. The primary evaluator and the academic professional should confer in developing their lists. While some names may appear on both lists, avoid complete duplication. The lists should provide the Dean with a substantial number of choices.

3. References may come from 3 areas: internal to the Libraries, within the ASU community and external to ASU. As the academic professional's career progresses, the expectation would be to have more references from the ASU community and from outside the University.

4. It is not expected that each referee will be able to address all areas of performance; however, each referee should be able to support one or more areas of the academic professional's job performance, professional development and/or service activities. Referees should be selected so that most of the academic professional's significant activities or achievements are addressed.

Letters of Reference Roster

Return to Librarians' Handbook main page

Page Compiled by: Librarians' Council
September 13, 2000
URL: http://www.asu.edu/lib/library/lc/handbook/G2_4.html

ASU Libraries: Architecture | Hayden | Law | Music | Polytechnic | Science | West

Contact Us
© Arizona Board of Regents

ASU ARIZONA STATE UNIVERSITY

OFFICE OF THE EXECUTIVE VICE PRESIDENT
AND PROVOST OF THE UNIVERSITY

Provost A-Z   a b c d e f g h i j k l m n o p q r s t u v w x y z   Directory Map eServices myASU

Home > Personnel Actions > **Information for Deans**

2004-2005 Schedule
Information for Deans
Information for all candidates

Downloads

DIRECTIONS FOR 2005-2006 PERSONNEL ACTIONS (TO DEANS)

Last Revision: 6/14/2005

Duplicate and distribute the personnel action calendar widely to all those who will be affected by it, including personnel committees, candidates, and secretaries.

Photocopy the page entitled MATERIALS TO BE SUBMITTED **and provide copies directly to candidates** for tenure (or continuing status for academic professionals) and promotion so that they will know what is to come forward to the university committee and to the Office of the Executive Vice President and University Provost. Draw their attention to the ability to make a statement (maximum of four pages) about their career goals and how their work ties together into an overall plan.

A current copy of the unit's/department's *approved* **promotion and tenure/continuing status review criteria needs to be included in the unit's/department's submission to the dean. The dean will then forward the unit/department criteria, as well as a current copy of the college's approved promotion and tenure review criteria, to the Office of the Executive Vice President and University Provost along with a cover memo listing the names of the candidate(s) file(s) to be reviewed.**

The unit's written criteria concerning evaluation for tenure and promotion must address evaluation issues pertaining to faculty who participate as affiliated faculty or as "core faculty" in another program, such as a department, center, institute, or interdisciplinary program. [See ACD 506-06]

With recent changes in ACD policy, probationary reviews for assistant professors (hired 2003/04 or thereafter) have been moved to third-year reviews (midway in their promotion and tenure review cycle); untenured associate professors (hired 2003/04 or thereafter) will continue to have their probationary reviews (midpoint) in their second year.

Be scrupulous in following the directions below for soliciting outside letters:

1. In comprising the list of external reviewers, half should be selected from the candidate's suggested reviewers and the other half from the chair/dean's suggested list of reviewers. *The unit head must consult with the dean in determining his/her list.*
2. Requests should be virtually the same for all candidates from a unit.
3. Requests should be written in neutral terms so as not to communicate that you are asking for either a negative or a positive endorsement. [See sample letter #1.] **Be sure to designate if the candidate is being reviewed for promotion only, tenure only, or both promotion and tenure.**
4. The packet of accompanying materials should be up-to-date and carefully prepared by the candidate (except for your letter) to present a well-rounded picture. It should resemble the packet that will come forward to the University Tenure and Promotion Committee (minus the evaluations),

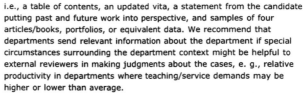

i.e., a table of contents, an updated vita, a statement from the candidate putting past and future work into perspective, and samples of four articles/books, portfolios, or equivalent data. We recommend that departments send relevant information about the department if special circumstances surrounding the department context might be helpful to external reviewers in making judgments about the cases, e. g., relative productivity in departments where teaching/service demands may be higher or lower than average.

5. A copy of the curriculum vitae of each reviewer should be included (if possible).

6. You should include a statement that the recommendations are confidential and will be seen only by appropriate administrators and reviewing committees. If your reviewing committee is made up of a large group, e.g., all faculty at rank and above, then explain the situation so that the writer will not be surprised at how many people read the evaluation. **This also means that internal recommendation letters should not identify the reviewers in any way (either by name, by description, by university affiliation, etc.).**

7. Send a "thank you for reviewing" letter to those who take the time to make a review. [See attached sample letter #3.]

Point #6 is extremely important. Current ACD policy allows faculty members or academic professionals to review their personnel file, with the exception of confidential references and external letters of evaluation. It is essential, therefore, that tenure/continuing status and promotion recommendations from personnel committees and others not include names, universities, or place of professional employment, nor descriptively identify the external reviewers in the letters of recommendation or reports.

Please ensure that names of external reviewers are listed ONLY on the grid entitled RECORD OF OUTSIDE LETTERS FOR ASU TENURE AND/OR PROMOTION. Please also provide additional narrative on the grid (Reason for Invitation/Professional Qualifications/Relationship to Candidate) as needed to contextualize the reviews. That is, for each evaluator, please describe the reviewer's qualifications, stature in the field, and area of expertise; provide enough detail so that reviewers outside of the discipline can make a fair determination about the weight to accord each review. All external reviewers should be listed on the grid even if they decline to review or do not respond with a review.

For further information about tenure/continuing status and promotion processes, refer to the 506 or 507 sections of the online ACD Manual, or contact Cecilia Hook if you have questions.

Search   Copyright   Accessibility   Privacy   Administration   Contact ASU

Office of the Executive Vice President and Provost of the University
Location: Foundation Building, Suite 420, 300 E. University Drive [Map]
Mail: PO Box 877805, Tempe, AZ 85287-7805
Phone: (480) 965-4995   Fax: (480) 965-0785

I. Review of Members of the Librarian Series
F. Review Initiator's Role

6. SOLICITATION OF LETTERS

    a. Letters are required in all accelerated reviews and in all cases where the candidate is being considered for promotion, accelerated advancement, career status, advancement to Librarian, Step VI, or termination.

    b. Letters may be solicited at the discretion of the Review Initiator in other cases as well, especially when the Review Initiator does not have firsthand knowledge of the candidate's performance in a certain area, when there is a likelihood that the candidate will not agree with the recommendation, or when no letters have been solicited for a review of the candidate in at least five years. When the Review Initiator exercises his or her discretion to solicit letters, the Review Initiator shall include the reason for soliciting letters in his or her letter of recommendation.

    c. When letters are to be solicited, the Review Initiator shall give the candidate an opportunity to suggest names of persons who are familiar with the candidate's performance. The candidate shall indicate the area(s) of performance about which the named persons might be particularly knowledgeable. Letters solicited by the Review Initiator shall include a reasonable number from the names provided by the candidate

    d. The candidate may also list names of persons who, for reasons set forth in writing, might not objectively evaluate, in a letter or on a committee, the candidate's qualifications or performance. Any such statement provided by the candidate shall be included in the review record. The Review Initiator may solicit letters from persons that the candidate has indicated might not be objective if the Review Initiator feels strongly that those persons would be appropriate. If this is the case, the review record must include both the candidate's statement indicating inappropriate referees and reasons for their inappropriateness and the Review Initiator's reasons for soliciting letters from them.

    e. Both the candidate's list and the Review Initiator's list shall become part of the review file.

    f. If the candidate is in a supervisory position, letters may be solicited from librarians in the supervisory chain below the candidate.

    g. The Review Initiator is not required to solicit letters from all individuals suggested by the candidate, nor is the Review Initiator restricted to that list of names. Indeed, the Review Initiator shall solicit letters from others when he/she deems them to be important sources for evaluation.

    h. The Review Initiator's request for a letter shall include the candidate's résumé; when evaluation of publications is sought, it is also helpful to include copies of publications not otherwise easily obtainable for the letter writer's reference. In addition, when soliciting letters from UCI librarians, the Review Initiator shall include the candidate's position profile(s) for the Criterion One period under review.

    i. All solicited letters received must be included in the review record, including communications in response to a solicitation which state that a letter will not be supplied.

I. Review of Members of the Librarian Series
F. Review Initiator's Role

11. CANDIDATE'S INSPECTION OF NON-CONFIDENTIAL DOCUMENTS

 a. Before forwarding the review record to the next review level, the Review Initiator shall provide the candidate the opportunity to inspect and make copies of all documents to be included in the review record other than confidential academic review documents. (Confidential academic review records are defined in Article 5, Personnel Files.)

 b. The Review Initiator shall provide a copy of his or her letter of recommendation to the candidate.

 MOU
 Article 4: Process for Merit Increase, Promotion and Career Status
    C. Procedures
       10, Before forwarding the academic review file to the next level of review, the review initiator shall provide the candidate an opportunity to inspect all documents to be included in the review file other than confidential academic review records as defined in Article 5, Personnel Files. A copy of the review initiator's letter of recommendation shall be provided to the candidate.

12. REDACTION FOR CANDIDATE OF CONFIDENTIAL DOCUMENTS

 a. Working with the Associate University Librarian for Administrative Services to ensure adherence to proper procedures, the Review Initiator shall provide to the candidate, upon written request, access to confidential academic review records. The records shall be subject to redaction as follows:

 1) For a letter of evaluation or statement from an individual evaluator, redaction shall consist of the removal of name, title, organizational/institutional affiliation, and relational information contained below the signature block of the letter of evaluation.

 2) Confidential individual letters of evaluation solicited from sources within the campus shall be included in the redaction as well as any outside letters.

 b. The Review Initiator shall give each letter writer an identification code and indicate the code on the form "Identification of Evaluators" (UCI-LIB-02). This alpha or numeric code must also be marked on the copied corresponding letter and must remain on the copied letter after it is redacted.

 c. Both the candidate's written request and redacted copies shall be included in the review file.

 d. The redacted copies shall be given to the candidate within seven calendar days, excluding University holidays, of receipt of the request .

 MOU
 Article 4: Process for Merit Increase, Promotion and Career Status
    C. Procedures
       11. The University shall provide to the candidate, upon written request, a redacted copy of the confidential documents included in the record.

Academic Personnel Procedures for Librarians: Represented Librarians   _page 37_
August 23, 2004

contents of the dossier.

Candidate's Responsibilities: The candidate is responsible for furnishing to the executive officer the information which is requisite for completing the forms and forwarding the case, but does not determine the content and presentation of the case. **The candidate will review the factual elements of the papers and acknowledge this review with a signature on the cover sheet. The executive officer has final responsibility and authority for the content and presentation of the papers.**

Candidate's Contributions (if any) to Collaborative Research (See Section V.C. of Part IV Forms).The letters in this section are to be solicited by the executive officer, **not** by the candidate. Unit **executive officers** are strongly encouraged to solicit letters from collaborators especially in multi-investigator studies.

The External Evaluation: In evaluating a candidate's scholarship, the department should obtain a written evaluation from **not fewer than 5 but no more than 8** members of the relevant profession(s) or discipline(s) who have not had a close association with the candidate.

Selection of Referees for the External Evaluation: Because the choice of outside references is critical to evaluating the candidates, the following guidelines should be observed:

Quality of Referees:

- Referees should be from strong departments at major research institutions, such as those typically found among Research I, AAU, or premier foreign institutions.

- All referees from universities must be full professors or equivalent (for example Readers at a British University) with outstanding scholarly accomplishment in the candidate's field.

- If referees are from industry or government, they should be of a similar stature to a full professor at a major research institution, and this should be justified in the papers.

Deviations from the above guidelines are permissible if a proper evaluation of the candidates work *would not otherwise be possible.* For example, if a candidate's field is so small that it will not be possible to find at least 5 referees satisfying the above criteria who have the expertise necessary to evaluate the candidate's work, if an Associate Professor is uniquely qualified to evaluate a candidate's work, or in situations where a faculty member is well known in the profession, it may be difficult to find leading scholars who do not have close ties with the candidate. Such deviations must be explained in detail. Simply saying "the field is too small" does not constitute a justification.

Objectivity and Conflicts of Interest:
- Referees should be chosen so that they will provide, and be seen to provide, evaluations that are as objective as possible. They should not have served as thesis advisor of the candidate, nor have collaborated with the candidate, nor have some other past or current close relationship with the candidate that would interfere with their objective assessment of the case, or give them a stake in the outcome of the case. However, as noted above, letters from collaborators which address a candidate's contribution to a collaboration may be solicited by the unit executive officer and included in Section V.C. in the P&T papers.

9

- Knowledge of the candidate (e.g., having heard the candidate speak at conferences, or being familiar with the candidate's work) does not constitute a conflict of interest, and indeed is evidence of the candidate's visibility and impact.

- Candidates may submit a list of referees who they believe **are inappropriate**, along with the reasons for their proposed exclusion. Though such a list is not binding, the executive officer making the final choice should take the proposed exclusions into account. **Candidates are, however, not allowed to submit to the department a list of potential referees.**

In view of the need for objectivity in evaluating a candidate's work, deviations from the guidelines on conflicts will not be permitted.

The solicitation of referees
It is recommended that this be done in two stages:

The first contact, which may be by e-mail, should inquire about the availability of the potential referee and willingness to serve, and must ask specifically whether the referee has been an advisor or collaborator with the candidate, or for any other reason might be seen as less than impartial. More than 8 potential referees may need to be contacted until a pool of at least 5 willing, objective, referees is assembled. **A list of all such contacts, with the responses (or lack thereof) is to be included with the papers.** Please see attached Sample A in Part III, Section 7B.

The second contact is the official letter. Please see attached Sample B in Part III, Section 7B.

Information that should be sent to referees in the second letter: All external referees should be sent copies of the candidate's updated curriculum vitae and a sample of recent publications (i.e., publications since the last personnel action) and work(s) in press. Where appropriate to the discipline, URL's for submissions to an electronic archive or online journal may be used instead of physical copies of the papers, if this is acceptable to the referee.

Solicitation of Letters: The solicitation of letters of evaluation should come from the executive officer or senior colleague who has been charged with preparing the documentation, never from the candidate. It should be clear that the purpose of the letter is to obtain a candid assessment of the candidate's scholarly accomplishments and standing in the field. Letters should indicate the rank for which the candidate is being considered and whether or not the award of tenure is involved. The tone of the letter should be neutral and should not indicate the desired outcome of the process. Solicitation letters to referees should **NOT** include language to suggest that the candidate can see the letters with the name and institution removed. Referees should be strongly encouraged to provide a critical evaluation and not merely summarize the candidate's c.v.

It is important to give adequate time for the referees to write their letters. Therefore, it is suggested that requests should be sent out as early as possible (e.g. by the end of May) in the year of consideration. All external evaluations of the nominee that were solicited by the department for the review must be included in the candidate's file even if the reviewer's letter is a simple statement of inability/unwillingness to review. Your solicitation letter should include the following (See Sample B, Part III, for full text):
In your letter would you please,

✓ *Note that you are evaluating the scholarship since the previous personnel action and not necessarily the number of calendar years. This is especially important in cases being*

10

reviewed for promotion to Associate Professor. Our campus has a tenure rollback policy that is granted on a case-by-case basis after review.•

✓ *Discuss the candidate's work in a critical fashion, commenting on the quality and impact of the candidate's scholarship.•*

✓ *Comment on the volume of the candidate 's scholarly activities relative to the standards in the field.•*

✓ *Remark on the quality of the publishing outlets and the source of funding when such is not obvious.•*

✓ *Estimate his/her standing in the field, and compare the candidate with other faculty of roughly the same cohort.•*

Please note that we do not ask you to make a recommendation regarding promotion itself, since that decision will be based partly on considerations such as teaching and service. Nor are we asking for a summary of the c.v.. What we seek is a substantive evaluation of the scholarly component of Dr._____ 's qualifications for promotion to the rank of _____. However, if you are in a position to comment on his/her teaching or other pertinent aspects of his/her professional activities, please feel free to do so.

Letters from Collaborators/Co-Authors: As indicated above, letters from co-authors that document the contributions of the candidate to co-authored work should NOT be included among the letters of evaluation. They should instead be solicited by the Executive Officer and included in Part V.C. of the Forms.

Where you cannot adhere to the above guidelines for securing letters of recommendation, please provide a the reason and an explanation of the process used in the papers. Cases in which there is evidence of a failure to secure an objective evaluation may prejudice the case and may lead to a call for future review.

Redacted Letters of Reference: UIC does not have a policy of permitting candidates to read external letters from referees. **Therefore, in the interest of uniformity and fairness, candidates will NOT be allowed to read letters of reference in any form.**

Translation of Letters of Reference: In the event that a translation of letters of reference is needed, the department should identify two persons to handle the translation; one to provide the translation and one to ensure the accuracy.

E-mail: External letters of evaluation must be signed by the writer. Letters sent by e-mail are not acceptable. **Original copies with a signature will need to be submitted with the candidate's papers.**

Confidentiality: **The identity of the referees must not be disclosed to the candidate,** nor should comments made in P&T deliberations be attributed to the faculty members who made them.

Based on the Supreme Court decision in the University of Pennsylvania case, as well as recent court decisions involving discrimination claims by faculty who have been denied

promotion and/or tenure, letters soliciting external reviews should state that the University shall maintain confidentiality of the identity of reviewer, **subject only to involuntary disclosure in legal proceedings.**

11

If teaching or service is the primary basis for the recommended promotion, the statement should reflect accomplishments and future plans in teaching or service and how they relate to research.

The departmental evaluation of research accomplishments should indeed be an evaluation, not merely a description of research. The emphasis should be placed on at least two publications or creative works. Of particular concern are the quality of execution, the significance of the topics, and the impact on the field.

The departmental evaluation of future potential has value only if it is developed in realistic terms. The discussion should focus on the candidate's strategy for developing his or her career as a scholar, and should include an assessment of the probable standing of the candidate within the subfield and larger discipline five years from the present.

Outside Evaluation of Research, Scholarship, Teaching, and Creative Activity

Letters from at least four scholars or professional specialists outside the University are required for each nominee. **These letters are critical components of the dossier and play a major role in the decision-making process.** The letters must be appropriate in several dimensions. They must be:

- sufficient in number,

- from appropriately selected individuals at **peer institutions**,
  (NOTE: If a unit has sought an evaluation from an individual outside of the university's peer ranks, an explanation must be provided. Letters from individuals not affiliated with a university but who are otherwise knowledgeable about standards and indicators of excellence that are meaningful in an academic environment at our level of achievement should be in addition to the four letters from evaluators at academic institutions.)

- from individuals of **appropriate** (usually senior) **rank**,

- from **objective evaluators** without conflicts of interest. For example, letters for tenure should not be solicited from the individual's thesis advisor or current or past collaborators.

- Date-stamped upon receipt.

Each evaluator should receive the candidate's dossier exclusive of evaluative materials and a representative sample of the candidate's scholarly or creative work. A single manuscript or creative work will rarely suffice as a representative sample.

Number of Letters. It is rare that more than six letters need be solicited. *All letters received must be included in the promotion papers. Likewise, a list of all those evaluators solicited must be included.* While it is appropriate for candidates to suggest persons

COMMUNICATION NO. 9

UNIVERSITY OF ILLINOIS • URBANA-CHAMPAIGN
OFFICE OF THE PROVOST

familiar with their work, *the departments must also seek letters from referees other than those suggested by the candidates.* Additional comments on this point are found below.

Department and Candidate Participation in Selection of Evaluators

Each candidate must be provided an opportunity to nominate external evaluators. The candidate's list of suggested external evaluators must include enough names to guarantee some degree of privacy to the evaluators. That is, the names must not be so few, nor the list so structured, that the candidate can, in effect, direct the inquiry toward particular individuals. **A majority of the external evaluations must come from the department's, rather than the candidate's, nominations.** These provisions suggest, in combination, that the unit request four to eight names from the candidate, that it solicit opinions from no more than two or three of the candidate's choices, and **that it obtain a slightly larger number of opinions from others.**

The candidate has no privilege of vetoing external reviewers, but may indicate individuals whom he or she considers inappropriately biased. The candidate cannot reasonably request avoidance of more than one or two individuals. It is the unit's responsibility to consider each such request seriously, but the unit is not bound to honor the request. If the questioned evaluator's opinion is deemed particularly relevant to the case, the unit may solicit an opinion.

Appropriate selection of evaluators. Be selective in choosing evaluators. Evaluators must be appropriate in several dimensions; they must be from appropriate institutions, in a position to comment upon the case from a perspective that will be informative to reviewing committees, and must be of appropriate rank.

Letters should be solicited only from outside evaluators who are in a position to comment in a discriminating and objective way on the nominee's current research or other professional work and should be from peer institutions which are used for other comparisons such as salaries. If the reviewers are not from peer institutions, please explain in the biographical sketch why the evaluator was chosen. In the campus committee, this matter is taken seriously. There are very good reasons for choosing evaluators from peer (or better) institutions, the principal ones being that such persons are more likely than others to share our standards for promotion and tenure and to understand the environment for scholarship.

The use of evaluators from industry or commerce, government agencies, or national laboratories should be limited for similar reasons. If such a person is used, his or her letter should not be part of the minimal group of four, but rather, *in addition to* the letters from evaluators in academe, and a clear statement should be made in the statement of the evaluator's qualifications about his or her knowledge of academic institutions, and why this individual was chosen.

UNIVERSITY OF ILLINOIS • URBANA-CHAMPAIGN
OFFICE OF THE PROVOST

Finally, it is expected that evaluators will normally be of a senior rank (full professor or equivalent) and never of a rank lower than the proposed rank of the candidate.

Objectivity of Evaluators. **Letters from close colleagues/collaborators, former professors, and mentors will very likely be discounted by the Campus Committee on Promotion and Tenure. Letters from such individuals are discouraged, essentially on grounds of conflict of interest.** If a department uses such an individual, the reasons for the extraordinary choice must be explained in the papers. In considering the use of "colleagues or collaborators" of the candidates, the guiding principle is to avoid recourse if the reviewer stands to benefit from the success of the reviewee. In general, one could expect that this would be true if the two shared a common grant, or were close collaborators on a number of common projects, for example. This phrase is not meant to exclude colleagues who have knowledge of the reviewee from ordinary professional contact in a community of scholars.

It is not appropriate to argue that a person cannot be evaluated except by a very small community, all of whom have a demonstrable conflict of interest of the kind described here. Scholarship of the quality that is to be recognized by promotion and tenure on this campus is expected to have substantial impact; that is, it must affect a community substantially larger than this sort of argument can admit.

Procedure for Soliciting Letters. Usually letters requesting an evaluation of the candidate's record are solicited by mail. This section describes language that must be used in the letters soliciting the evaluation. Some departments choose to make prior telephone contact with potential reviewers to ascertain the referee's willingness to provide a review of a candidate. When this type of contact is made, it is essential that neutrality about the candidate be maintained in the telephone conversation in the manner required in the written request to provide a review. If the reviewer agrees, the letter of confirmation should include the required language outlined below. In cases where the contacted party declines to serve as a reviewer, the name of the individual contacted must be included with the list of referees (section VI. B) and the reason for declining the request should be provided.

A copy of the letter or letters of solicitation must be in the recommendation package. (If the same letter was sent to several different individuals, only one of the letters of solicitation need be submitted.) **It is extremely important that these letters reflect the exacting standards for promotion and tenure at our institution.**

Required Elements

Neutrality. Letters to outside referees must not include passages such as "We have decided to recommend the promotion of . . ." or "Will you please help us to make a case for . . ." or "We are very pleased with X; she is an excellent . . ." Such phrases are likely to bias the response of the outside referee, for they present the evaluator with the appearance of a fait accompli. These letters should be written in a neutral fashion: "We are considering recommending Assistant Professor X for promotion," or "Your comments are requested and will be used to help us decide . . ." The letters soliciting outside evaluation should request, if possible, an in-depth analysis of the candidate's performance and national stature rather than an overall impression. Thus letters of solicitation should include a phrase akin to the following:

> Please provide us with your analysis of the significance of Professor _____'s work within the canon. It would also be most useful for us if you could provide some comparisons of Professor _____ with her (his) peers.

Rank. Letters to referees should indicate the rank to which the candidate is being considered for promotion. If the promotion considered is to associate professor, the letter should state that the considered action involves promotion with indefinite tenure. In the case of a "Q" appointee for whom one is soliciting a letter about the granting of tenure without promotion, it is important to specify that the candidate is being considered for "indefinite tenure without change in rank."

Additional Authorities. The letter to each external evaluator must include the following required language concerning additional authorities:

The Provost of our campus requests that you provide, in addition to your own comments about this case, the names of two or three other authorities who might be consulted about it.

Confidentiality. The letter must also include a statement that the confidentiality of the referee's remarks will be protected to the extent possible within the law. The following language is required:

The policy of the University of Illinois is to hold in confidence all letters of evaluation from persons outside the institution. Only the committees and administrative officers directly responsible for the decision of concern here will have access to your letter. It will not be provided to the person on whom you comment unless we are compelled by law **to do so.**

Procedure for Providing Information on Evaluators. The qualifications, including academic ranks or titles and current affiliation, of all outside evaluators must be provided in the promotion papers. The evaluators should be well known in the field; it is generally *not* appropriate to ask the evaluator to provide a curriculum vitae along with his or her letter of response. If the basis for evaluation is not indicated in the letter of evaluation, please identify why the evaluator is writing the letter (i.e., in what way does the evaluator know the nominee and his or her work) and report any direct relationship (e.g., post-doctoral supervisor, co-investigator, or co-author) between the evaluator and the candidate. To avoid non-response, departments may wish to request letters of evaluation as early as the preceding spring. Negative comments in letters should be addressed (not just dismissed as unfair) by the department head since they are sure to attract attention in the course of the review process. In order to distinguish those referees suggested by the candidate from those chosen by the department, please type after the referee's name in the biographical sketch either (chosen by the candidate) or (chosen by the department). If an outside evaluator does not respond, briefly indicate the reason, if known.

Other Notes

"Early" Promotion of an Assistant Professor

An assistant professor may be considered for promotion and tenure in any year before the sixth year of the probationary period. Although promotion before the sixth year may be warranted in some cases, early promotion should not be the norm; it requires evidence of truly outstanding accomplishments and unusual potential. The executive officer's comments should include an explanation of why early promotion is in the interest of the University. The term "early" here is meant only to designate a review that occurs before it is actually mandated by the University's regulations; it does not imply a reluctance by the campus to consider such a case.

The early consideration of assistant professors for promotion and tenure presents some hazards and must be handled delicately. Failure to promote exceptional people could seriously affect our ability to recruit and to retain first-rate faculty members. There may be a significant institutional benefit in terms of loyalty and job satisfaction when clearly outstanding young staff are encouraged and rewarded before they have received an offer to go elsewhere. On the other hand, college and campus committees will demand evidence that an early promotion recommendation is compelling. Denial of early promotion can lead to disappointment and disaffection on the part of the faculty member. Thus, premature recommendations, even of strong candidates, may have exactly the opposite effect from that desired. Departments should therefore proceed carefully and thoughtfully in considering such cases and should avoid arousing expectations that may not be satisfied.

Promotions of Nontenure-track Faculty

Individuals with faculty rank but not on the tenure track, including those on clinical, adjunct, research, or zero percent-time faculty appointments, may be nominated for promotion in two different ways. One is to follow the process for tenure-track faculty, as outlined elsewhere in this Communication. This approach is best suited to candidates whose responsibilities closely parallel the activities of tenure-track faculty members. The other avenue is an administrative review process not requiring consultation with the Campus Committee on Promotion and Tenure. This second process is briefly described in this section.

The general principles of excellence in scholarship, reflective evaluation, and two-level review should apply to all cases of proposed promotion. Each college in which such

VI. External Evaluations
A. Sample Letter(s) to External Evaluators
B. Qualifications of the External Evaluators
C. Letters from External Evaluators

VII. Special Comments by the Executive Officer

Appendix 2 Internal and External referees
Internal referees:

- Dean of College served
- Head of Department served
- Chair or member of Library Committee
- Users of the library
- Faculty served
- * Librarians from non-peer institutions
- * Librarians from other divisions

External referees:

- Colleagues (librarians) at peer institutions
- Chair of committee in ALA, SLA, MLA, or other professional organization on which candidate has served
- Other professional organization officers, etc.
- NOT APPROPRIATE: co-authors or individuals with whom the candidate formerly worked

Lists of external referees should be accompanied by a short statement why this individual is qualified to serve. Curriculum vitae or lists of publications may
accompany these lists.
* For units without a defined constituency

Appendix 3 Possible areas of review to discuss with referees
Peer Review Committees gather information relating to librarianship with individuals within the Library and UIUC non-library faculty.
Areas of evaluation: Solicit Evaluative Comments from:

1. **Reference service and user education:** Library users; unit head or division (Including reference, computer-based services, coordinator; departmental faculty and instruction, excluding formal courses)
2. **Selection and Preservation:** (Selection of books, journals, and other materials: Library users, unit head or division members; Preservation: collection coordinator, departmental faculty, departmental library committee chair; collection development chair
3. **Management and budgetary activities:** Unit head or division coordinator; executive officer(s) of academic department(s) or college; departmental library committee chair
4. **Intellectual/ Bibliographic control:** Unit head or division coordinator; individuals with cataloging responsibilities
5. **Systems activities:** Unit head or division coordinator, systems librarian, building network administrator
6. **Special projects and/or other assignments:** Unit head or division coordinator, other appropriate individuals
7. **Library/University service:** Unit head or division coordinator, committee chair or members

Appendix 4 Guidelines for Interviewing Internal Referees
During these scheduled interviews, the Peer Review Committee is expected to:

1. state that the purpose of the interview is to assess candidate's progress towards research, service and librarianship during the probationary period. THIS IS NOT TENURE REVIEW.
2. review procedures and discuss the significance of formal evaluation
3. state that this conversation is confidential
4. identify that this will be an oral evaluation only, but extensive, adequate typed notes will be retained for files
5. review the goals and objectives of the candidates job incorporating the following factors:
   o professional competency and creativity
   o overall relationship with library personnel and clientele and/or liaison department faculty and students
   o commitment to the library profession
   o communication skills

- strengths and weaknesses
6. assess referee's willingness to be placed on a list of referees to be contacted at promotion time.

(If significant reservations are expressed about any area of job performance, Peer Review Committee members should strongly urge that the appropriate library administrator address these issues with the candidate explicitly, providing specific suggestions as to how performance might be improved.)

Appendix 5

NOTE: This letter is to be issued by the University Librarian's Office, **not** by members of PRC.

An email message to external evaluators asking whether they would be willing to serve as external evaluators should be sent by members of the PRC. This will be followed by an official letter from the University Librarian's Office to those willing to serve as external reviewers.

Sample request to external referees regarding candidate's research and scholarship in 3Y and beyond

Dear Prof. Appletree:

I am on the Peer Review Committee (a review committee) for Professor Albert Einstein that will be undertaking a formal review of his progress in the third year of his probationary period. The procedures at the University of Illinois require formal external evaluations of tenure-track faculty at intermediate points in their career. This evaluation is being conducted to inform the candidate and the University of strengths and weaknesses that may have an impact on the future tenure decision.

I am asking you to assist us by evaluating Professor Einstein's record in scholarship and contributions to the profession by evidence of valuable leadership and service. I am enclosing Professor Einstein's vita, as well as a recent offprint(s) for your convenience. It would be most helpful if you would refer to specific items in your assessment.

The Peer Review Committee would be grateful for your prompt response to this request which should be addressed to me. Our deadline for receipt of your evaluation (by fax: , by e-mail, or letter) is ---------. Since we realize that your thoughtful review and evaluation of our colleague will require careful consideration, if you are UNABLE to do so at this time, would you please advise me at your earliest convenience.

The policy of the University of Illinois is to hold in confidence all letters of evaluation. Only the committees and administrative officers directly responsible for the tenure process will have access to your comments. It will not be provided to the candidate unless we are required specifically and legally to do so.

Sincerely,

Appendix 6

Possible questions for use by Peer Review Committee when interviewing internal referees:

Reference and Information Service

1. When at work, is the librarian available to assist users?
2. Is the librarian approachable to users?
3. How would you rate your level of satisfaction in finding the information you need through this person?
4. Does the librarian show initiative in offering professional help?
5. In your opinion, what is the librarian's level of knowledge in respect to various information sources relating to your field of expertise?
6. Does the librarian show innovative approaches to the provision of service?
7. Have you attended any instructional sessions conducted by this librarian? If yes, how would you rate the value of the same?
8. Generally speaking, how would you rate the librarian's communication skills?
9. What is your overall opinion as the librarian's professional competency in the area of reference service?

Collection Development

1. In your opinion, does the librarian keep abreast of research and current developments in your field of expertise?
2. Are you satisfied that the librarian is doing everything possible to identify and acquire materials published in your field of expertise?
3. Does the librarian respond to faculty/user suggestions regarding materials for acquisition?
4. In the event of the library not being able to acquire requested material, are you satisfied with the librarian's explanation or suggestion for an alternative means of acquiring the same material?
5. In your opinion, is the librarian helpful to users in regard to specific inquiries (such as following up on book orders already placed, making inquiries concerning items in binding, etc.)?
6. Does the library acquire recently published materials in your area of expertise in a timely manner?
7. Allowing for the fact that library budgets and collection development policies do not usually permit comprehensive acquisition in any single are, do you consider that the librarian is making appropriate choices of items to purchase out of the entire range of material published in your field of expertise?
8. What is your overall impression of the librarian's performance in respect to building the collection generally?

Management and Administration

1. In your opinion, does the librarian strive to meet the research and teaching needs of the departmental clientele served?
2. Is the general atmosphere of the library "user friendly?"
3. How often do you use the library?
4. Is the librarian open to dialogue? Does the librarian effectively communicate the library's policies and services to users?
5. What, in your opinion, are the positive aspects of the librarian's performance?
6. Do you perceive any problem areas in the way in which the librarian performs assigned duties? If so, please describe:
7. Does the librarian handle the budget effectively?
8. Does the librarian display effective skills in time management and delegation of responsibilities?
9. Does the librarian encourage the professional development of colleagues and staff?

Bibliographic Control
What are your observations and perceptions as to the librarian's job performance in respect to:

1. Accuracy
2. Productivity
3. Knowledge of cataloging theory and practice
4. Keeping abreast of changes in rules and conventions
5. Development and utilization, as appropriate, of non-traditional approaches.

Appendix 7 Archival Files
Archival files should be maintained by members of the Peer Review Committee for the probationary period only and should contain:

- all documents the candidate submits to the Peer Review Committee, including "Outline for Promotion Dossier"
- all previous Peer Review Committee reports
- other notes, names of internal and external references, and any other information gathered by the Peer Review Committee

Upon completion of the probationary term or termination of employment at the university, these files will be transferred to the University Librarian's office.

Appendix 8
Instructions to candidates responding to the Peer Review Committee Report

1. If you are concerned with written comments made by your Peer Review Committee in your annual evaluation, please contact the members of your Peer Review Committee to arrange a meeting to clarify any misunderstandings or misconceptions. Conversely, if you are pleased with your report, this is an appropriate vehicle for so stating.
2. After meeting with your Peer Review Committee, if you feel that your accomplishments in the area/s of Librarianship, Service and/or Research and Publication, have not been represented accurately, please respond to your Peer Review Committee with a written clarification. Your response should take into account any extenuating circumstances not recognized in the Peer Review Committee report such as administrative hardships in your unit and personality conflicts within the unit, etc.

Appendix 9
Special Problems
If the Peer Review Committee has concerns that there is a serious impediment to achieving tenure which is deemed to be beyond the control of the candidate (whether it be for administrative reasons, personnel issues, etc.), the Committee may contact the Chair of FRC (in written form). The Chair of FRC may convene the Committee to determine the appropriate course of action.

The untenured faculty member may contact the Chair of FRC to alert the Committee of a potential obstacle to achieving tenure. FRC will seek consultation, if appropriate with the University Librarian or his/her designated representative.

B. Evaluation of Research, Scholarship, Creative or Artistic Performance

Guidelines for External Evaluations

The purpose of external peer evaluations is to provide an <u>independent,</u> <u>unbiased</u> evaluation of the candidate's scholarly attainment in the discipline. Comments and reviews by outside scholars and professionals in the same discipline or performance area shall be provided as part of the material forwarded to UCPT. All files are expected to contain 6 external evaluations. In exceptional cases, the number may be less than 6, but never fewer than 4 evaluations. *The department must provide a justification for files with less than 6 evaluations.*

NOTE: The solicitation process for external evaluations should begin in sufficient time to confirm and receive six evaluations providing thorough appraisals of the candidate's work. <u>All</u> evaluations solicited and received are required to be included in the file.

> *Identification of Reviewers*

The school or department is responsible for making every effort to obtain qualified evaluators who can provide fair and objective assessments of the candidate's work.

Qualifications of Evaluators: It is expected that outside evaluators will hold a rank at a level at least <u>equal</u> to the rank to which the candidate is seeking promotion at an institution comparable to KU or have comparable professional standing in a non-academic setting. Evaluators should possess credentials that will document their expertise in evaluating the candidate's work within the context of the discipline or profession.

Objectivity: One criterion in determining the degree of objectivity of external evaluators is the nature of the relationships with the candidate. Therefore, external evaluators must not include individuals who have a close academic or personal connection with the candidate (for example, dissertation advisors, former professors, graduate school colleagues, co-authors, KU faculty, personal friends, one's own former students, etc.). In rare cases, the candidate's specialized research or very narrow, specialized field of expertise requires drawing from individuals with close professional connections. In these instances, the unit is responsible for <u>explaining</u> and <u>justifying</u> an exception to this requirement. This justification should be transmitted to the UCPT.

While the University does not have a standardized university-wide selection procedure, all department/School processes must meet the following guidelines:

- The department is responsible for using its judgment in the final selection of external evaluators. Candidates must not themselves solicit recommendations, nor must they provide recommendations or evaluations for themselves.

- The candidate should be asked to provide up to 4 names of potential external evaluators; and may identify up to 2 individuals who they prefer to not be reviewers.

- The criteria and process for selection of external evaluators must be communicated to the candidate.

xvii

> *Confidentiality of*
> *External Reviews*

Policies governing the confidentiality of external evaluations are established by the schools and the College. The decision concerning confidentiality will not be delegated below the College or School administrative level. UCPT should be apprised of the School and College policy at the annual meeting with the Academic Deans. All letters to external evaluators must disclose the College or School policy.

>*Required Statements*

Confidential

"As a part of the promotion and/or tenure review process, we are soliciting assessments of Professor_____'s research contributions from academic colleagues and distinguished professionals. These letters will become part of the candidate's promotion and tenure dossier and are treated as confidential by the University to the extent we are permitted to do so by law."

Not confidential

"As a part of the promotion and/or tenure review process, we are soliciting assessments of Professor_____'s research contributions from academic colleagues and distinguished professionals. These letters will become part of the candidate's promotion and tenure dossier."

> *Evaluation Focus*

Evaluators should be sent an appropriately representative body of the candidate's work to review. The candidate should have input into the selection of work to be sent. Evaluators should be requested to review and evaluate the quality of the candidate's work, including published materials and any work submitted for publication or completed and ready for submission.

All letters to external evaluators must contain the following: School/College confidentiality statement, a request for a short form of the individual's CV, and identification of the following evaluation areas which must be addressed by the evaluator at a minimum:

1) Length and capacity of his/her association with the candidate;
2) The quality of the candidate's work;
3) The significance of the candidate's work to the discipline/profession
4) The pattern of productivity reflected in the candidate's record compared to discipline characteristics
5) The level of state, regional, national and/or international stature of the candidate as a result of this work;
6) Any special distinction achieved by the candidate

1. External Evaluation of Research, Scholarship, Creative or Artistic Performance *

(Page 20)

>*Accompanying Documentation*

The following materials must be enclosed with this section of the form:

- One copy of the letter requesting evaluations from outside scholars or professionals;
- Copies of all responses to requests (including declines and explanations of non-responses); original or faxed letters on official letterhead and signed are required for all external evaluations. **Electronic Submission of External Letters:** Any e-mail letter included in the file instead of the required signed hard copy must be accompanied by a departmental e-

xviii

mail requesting submission of a hard copy with signature.
- List of materials sent to each evaluator;
- A brief biographical statement establishing the scholarly reputation of each external evaluator and identification of the relationship of the evaluator to the candidate; and
- Evaluators' vita (short form)

The biographical statement and accompanying vita should indicate to UCPT the individual's status/stature in the discipline or profession, why this individual has the credentials to assess the candidate's research, scholarship, or creative activity, why they were selected as reviewers, and if they have a personal or academic connection with the candidate.

Evaluator Selection Process

1.a. A statement of the school or department's procedure for identifying and selecting evaluators must be provided. The procedures for replacing reviewers who withdraw after agreeing to participate and for transmitting the criteria and selection procedure to the candidate are also to be addressed in this section.

Justification for < 6 letters

1.b. If less than six evaluation letters are included in the file, a justification must be provided in this section.

(Page 21)

1.c. List in chronological order all individuals contacted to be external reviewers. Indicate their position/title, the date the request was made, whether they agreed to provide an evaluation, and the date the evaluation was received. Indicate with an asterisk (*) evaluators recommended by the candidate.

> *Location of Materials in Dossier*

◆ *Required Evaluations*

All letters solicited and received from external reviewers identified in 1.b. must be placed in the separate file folder (Folder D) labeled "Record and Evaluation of Research/Creative Activity." Copies of all letters requesting the evaluations are to be placed in this folder. While six evaluations are expected, in no case should fewer than four letters be submitted in the file.

The vita and brief biographical statement for each reviewer should precede the response of each evaluator.

ONLY evaluations requested by the unit for the purpose designated in this section of the form should be included in Folder D of the dossier.

NOTE: These evaluations remain a part of the permanent promotion and tenure dossier.

◆ *Other Support Letters*

All other letters of evaluation or support and other relevant data, etc., should be clearly labeled as such and placed in folders (Folders G, . . .). Folders containing solicited letters should be clearly labeled and a copy of the solicitation letter, which must include the School/College confidentiality policy, should be placed in the folder. A clear distinction should be made between the content of this solicitation letter and the external reviewer letter in Folder D of the dossier.

xix

2. Evaluation of Research, Scholarship, Creative and Artistic Performance

Qualitative Evaluation *

Evaluate each item (since the last promotion) on in Sections IV.A.3 (a) and (b), pages 13-15 according to the procedures described on page 12. Use the following rating scale:

E = Exceptional; VG=Very Good; G = Good; M = Marginal; P = Poor

(Page 21)

In this section of the form, separate comments may be provided regarding significant presentations, consulting activities, and external and internal funding awards.

(Page 22)

3. Expectations in Field and Overall Quality

Field Expectations *

The research/scholarship/creative work of the candidate and its quality is evaluated in relation to school or departmental expectations. The evaluation should include any statements that will assist the UCPT in its evaluation of the contribution of the candidate to the particular field of study or discipline.

Special information deemed necessary to establish the quality of the candidate's research, scholarship, creative or artistic performance may be provided through outside letters or statements. Such statements may include such matters as standards of the discipline, level of involvement of the candidate in a project, the expectations for and role of collaborative research, descriptions of specialized evaluation strategies, such as special peer review panels of specific work. Letters or statements solicited in support of the evaluation process must be labeled as such and placed in Folder G.

4. Overall Research, Scholarship, Creative, or Artistic Performance

Overall Rating of Research, Scholarship, Creative, or Artistic Performance *

Mark the appropriate category reflecting an overall rating of the research, scholarship or creative artistic performance of the candidate. The full range of the scale should be considered when judging the candidate's performance.

E = Exceptional; VG=Very Good; G = Good; M = Marginal; P = Poor

The final judgment should reflect the evaluations included in this section and the accompanying documentation. This rating should reflect a critical assessment of the content, significance, quality and quantity of the candidate's research, scholarly or creative activity and the extent to which the work has earned the candidate regional or national recognition, as appropriate. Provide comments describing the basis for this rating.

If there is a vote on individual ratings, please show the distribution of votes for each rating.

Provide the rationale for the rating under comments.

For recommendations for promotion to full professor, national and/or international stature of the candidate should be indicated, where applicable, and the basis for this assessment should be included.

>>>>>>>>>>

xx

Appendix III: External Review Procedures

Promotions from Assistant Professor to Associate Professor and from Associate Professor to Professor require external review of research and creative activity. Expert, objective, external reviewers will be asked to evaluate the quality and impact of the contribution of the research and creativity of the candidate for promotion.

The reviewers shall:
- o have a rank or position at the same level or higher in a professional position relevant to the candidate's position.
- o be neutral and may not be more than casual acquaintances of the candidate. Reviewers may have served on professional association committees with the candidate, but they must not have been professional collaborators (e.g., co-worker or co-author on an article or grant).

Three external reviewers will be selected using the following procedure:
- o The candidate will submit to the University Libraries Faculty Personnel Committee names of up to five external colleagues considered qualified to act as reviewers of submitted material.
- o If the candidate submits less than five names, the Personnel Officer will submit however many names necessary to bring the pool to five potential reviewers. The reviewers submitted by the Personnel Officer will be selected on the basis of similarity to the candidate's job position, rank sought, and institution. The reviewers will be solicited from the faculty of benchmark institutions (as designated by the University of Louisville Office of Planning and Budget) or from the faculty of comparable institutions.
- o The University Libraries Faculty Personnel Committee will select three reviewers.
- o The candidate shall have the opportunity to review the list and eliminate anyone for cause, including any with whom they have a personal relationship. The candidate must certify in writing that the reviewers meet the criteria of neutrality stated above.
- o The Committee Chair will invite the three to serve as reviewers.

Reviewers who have agreed to serve will receive the following materials from the University Libraries Faculty Personnel Committee:
- o a copy of the candidate's resumé,
- o a copy of the Minimum Guidelines' section on External Evaluation,
- o and the material to be reviewed.

The candidate must approve the contents of the review package and may include appropriate material, including but not limited to:
- o scholarly publications
- o reviews
- o notes/slides from presentations
- o grant proposals
- o reports (professional committee, projects)
- o computer programs (with appropriate text).

External reviewers will not be asked for a recommendation for promotion, nor will their recommendations be considered if given. Their opinions of the material will be given due consideration in the University Libraries Faculty Personnel Committee's promotion procedure. The University Libraries Faculty Personnel Committee will provide a written analysis of the validity and significance of the reviews received.

The candidate will be notified when all external reviews have been received. The candidate will have five working days in which to request to see the reviews and another five working days in which to submit a written response to the University Libraries Faculty Personnel Committee. This response will be included in the materials to be reviewed by the University Libraries Faculty Personnel Committee for consideration during the promotion procedure.

Document as approved by ULF on December 7, 2004

University of Louisville Minimum Guidelines
Excerpt on External Evaluations

External evaluation is required for research and creative activity in tenure and promotion review. These evaluations shall be conducted under standards and procedures specified in the unit document under these minimum guidelines:

a.   Each unit document must specify the process by which external evaluators shall be solicited. This process shall be designed to certify the professional expertise and objectivity of the evaluators, whose comments regarding the quality of the work under review shall be solicited along with justification of those comments.

b.   The person being reviewed shall have the opportunity to respond in writing to extramural evaluations. This response must be included in the review materials prior to consideration of the evaluation by any reviewing person or body. Each unit shall establish appropriate procedures for the accomplishment of these ends.

c.   The opinions of extramural evaluators shall be given due weight. but external evaluators' recommendations as to the award of tenure or promotion shall not be solicited nor considered if offered. The unit personnel committee shall provide a written analysis of the validity and significance of the evaluations received.

ATTACHMENT B

UNIVERSITY LIBRARIES,
UNIVERSITY OF NEBRASKA-LINCOLN
Preparing an External Review Portfolio
February 2005

A candidate's external review portfolio for promotion and/or continuous appointment is sent to the external reviewers. This portfolio is designed to provide the reviewers with information adequate for them to evaluate the candidate's work. Reviewers are asked to provide their expert advice on the nature and extent of the candidate's contributions and on the quality, significance, impact, and potential of his/her work. The portfolio as a whole does not become part of the promotion and/or continuous appointment documentation, though copies of some of the documents will be included in the documentation.

The University Libraries external portfolio consists of the following documents and items:

1. A letter from the Dean of Libraries or designee to the external reviewer explaining the expectations of the reviewers and providing information on the format of the review and the date by which the letters are to be sent to the Libraries.
2. A copy of the waiver form.
3. The candidate's nomination statement for promotion or continuous appointment.
   This statement briefly outlines the reasons for the nomination.
4. The candidate's statement identifying the candidate's work that in the candidate's judgment is most significant, and points out what its impact has been or will be.
   It is suggested that this statement speak specifically to each of the three criteria in the order outlined in the University Libraries Promotion and Continuous Appointment Criteria. These criteria are 1) Performance in assigned areas of responsibility, 2) Scholarly/creative activities, and 3) Service/Outreach to the University Libraries, the University, the profession, and the public.
5. Current Curriculum Vitae. This is prepared by the candidate and is a copy of the vitae that will go into the candidate's promotion and continuous appointment folders.
6. Relevant position descriptions(s).
   If the candidate's areas of responsibility have changed considerably during the period being reviewed, a position description for each major change should be included with the date.
7. Copies of selected refereed and other significant publications.
8. Other selected significant documentation.

The University states that an administrative unit's criteria for continuous appointment and promotion are not to be included in the external review portfolio.

The external reviewer is not asked whether the candidate should or should not receive tenure. This is a decision for the library faculty and the review process. The decision must reflect the particular institutional circumstances of the University of Nebraska.

Nothing can be added to the external review portfolio without the knowledge of the candidate. The candidate has a right to review, object to, and respond in writing to any added materials with the response becoming a part of the file.

UNIVERSITY LIBRARIES
UNIVERSITY OF NEBRASKA-LINCOLN

Waiver of Right to See Information

I am aware of Part II of the UNL **Policy on Rights of Access and Materials Used in Personnel Evaluation**. I am aware that I may waive my rights guaranteed by the Bylaws, but that the waiver may not be assumed, implied or required.

Signature _____

Date _____

I waive my right of access to information regarding the recommendations about my **Continuous Appointment and Promotion File** as follows (check and initial):

_____   I do not waive any of my rights of access to evaluate information solicited from outside reviewers, and have the right to inspect the reviews and submit a written response.

_____   I waive the right to know the identity of the outside reviewers, but reserve the right to examine the written comments they have submitted, and have the right to submit a written response.

_____   I waive the right to inspect all written comments solicited from outside peer reviewers and to know the identity of the outside reviewers.

When outside reviews are solicited, the exact nature of the waiver of rights checked above will be communicated to the reviewer and to any individuals or committee making promotion and/or continuous appointment recommendations.

Signature _____

Date _____

COARTwaiver
04-19-00--JBF

CONTENTS AND EVALUATION OF EACH TENURE/PROMOTION PACKET

To ensure that the best possible case is made for each candidate and that the evaluation of all candidates is conducted on an equitable basis across the University, each tenure/promotion packet should contain the materials specified below. Based on the data and information listed below, the academic unit is asked to evaluate the candidate's performance in teaching, research or creative activities, and service; to document that evaluation; and to indicate how the candidate's expertise is expected to contribute to the short- and long-range educational goals of the academic unit, college, and the University.

The forms attached to this memorandum should be completed for each candidate and should appear in the order indicated on the **"Dossier Checklist."** The Campus Tenure Committee recommends labeled index tabs to clearly identify each section within a dossier. (Available to be downloaded at http://www.ou.edu/provost/pronew/content/tenandpromomenu.html. Please follow the sequence and numbering on the dossier checklist. Brevity is encouraged. A 2-3 page summary of research is, in most cases, preferable to including copies of actual research publications in the dossier. Nevertheless, the candidate has the right to include anything in the dossier that he/she wishes. If included, copies of research publications should be in an appendix at the end of the dossier so as not to obscure other required components of the dossier.

Part I: Procedures and Evaluation

1.   The <u>cover</u> <u>sheet</u> for each packet is the completed **"Summary of Recommendation Concerning Tenure/Promotion."** It provides a useful summary of data concerning the candidate, information about the academic unit, and the vote of the eligible faculty. While the unit is asked to complete this form, the Dean is expected to verify the completeness and accuracy of the data.

Also note the following:

A.   **The definitions of a vote coded to** grant **or** deny **are self-evident. A vote coded as** abstain **means that an eligible faculty member reviewed the dossier, participated in the eligible faculty discussion and elected to cast a vote of abstain; i.e., they do not want to make either a positive or negative recommendation. However, it is difficult for others who review the dossier to consider a vote to abstain as a completely neutral vote; some individuals interpret it as mildly negative.**

A vote coded unavailable **means that an eligible faculty member did not review the dossier nor participate in the eligible faculty discussion and voting process. This happens most typically when a faculty member is on sabbatical and out of the country. A vote coded** ineligible **means that an otherwise eligible faculty member is recusing themselves from casting a vote. This most typically occurs when the candidate is a spouse of the eligible faculty member.**

The eligible faculty vote, in order to be considered positive, should have a majority of the votes coded grant as compared to the total number of votes coded grant, deny, and abstain. Ineligible and unavailable votes should not be used in computing the percentage.

B.   A recommendation to Promote requires a majority decision of all those voting, including those abstaining. Votes may only be to Promote, Not Promote,

Abstain, Unavailable, or Ineligible. AT LEAST FULL PROFESSORS VOTE. Chair/Directors should append a copy of the unit's policy on promotion votes and a list of faculty eligible to vote.

C.   For faculty seeking Tenure/Promotion who are budgeted in two or more units, the full numerical results of the votes by the academic units shall be reported and fully considered. However, in characterizing the overall vote at the unit level as positive or negative, the Provost and Campus Tenure Committee will weigh the overall positive or negative result of each unit by the percent of the candidate's salary contributed by that unit during the current year. Thus, for a candidate whose salary is evenly split between two units and who receives a positive vote in one unit and a negative vote in the other, the vote will be characterized as evenly split regardless of the absolute numbers of faculty voting positively or negatively.

2.   The Summary of Recommendation pages should be followed by a description of the **procedures** the unit used for the tenure/promotion process. A sample of such a procedure statement follows:

SAMPLE

Procedural Details of Faculty Vote on Tenure and Promotion

The tenure dossier of Professor XX was compiled and made available for inspection to the (number) tenured faculty in the Department of Art & Automation on October 14, 20__. (Note here if any tenured faculty were ineligible to vote due to the nepotism policy or for other reasons). The tenured faculty met to discuss Professor XX's qualifications on October 28, 20__*, with 13 of the 15 tenured faculty members in the department present (absent were Professor YY and Associate Professor ZZ). At the conclusion of this meeting ballots were distributed with instructions that they be completed and returned by no later than 5:00 p.m. on October 28, 20__. Completed ballots were deposited in a ballot box and the voting faculty member's name was checked off on a list of the department's tenured faculty. Professor YY submitted an absentee ballot; we were not able to obtain a vote from Professor ZZ, who is on sabbatical. The Chair and Committee A met on October __, 20__ to tally the tenure and promotion votes for Professor XX. At this same meeting, Committee A conducted its vote by a show of hands, and subsequently the Chair advised Committee A of their vote.

*Note the two-week period for inspection of the dossier as specified in the *Faculty Handbook*. Exceptions to this procedure should be noted, and approval for such exceptions should be obtained from the unit's tenured faculty, college dean, and University Senior Vice President and Provost, as appropriate.

3.   **The Unit Tenure Guidelines should follow.**

4.   **For tenure candidates, the next page of the packet is the "Recommendation of Committee A" (including minority reports, if any) with critical assessments of the quality, quantity, and significance in Teaching and Advising, Research and Creative Activity, and Service. Provide an analysis of how the candidate meets or does not meet the unit tenure guidelines, and discussions in the light of tenure cases in the recent past.**

For promotion candidates, the next page of the packet is the "Recommendation of Committee A" (with the individual vote of each member recorded) as required by Regents' policy, which provides that each member record an independent opinion, by name, without obligation to represent majority departmental opinion. Individual members may submit separate reports, that is, each member must record his/her own vote by name, and also has the option of submitting a separate report articulating the reasons for their decision.

5. The next page of the packet is the **"Recommendation of the Chair/Director"** (with supporting reasons).

    It is essential that all these recommendations specify how the candidate fulfills the unit's and University's criteria for tenure and/or promotion in the areas of Teaching and Advising, Research and Creative Activity, and Service. If the candidate to be considered has been hired with special stipulations or exceptions with regard to the unit's criteria for tenure and/or promotion, such conditions should be explicitly stated in the packet.

6. The **"Recommendation of the College Dean"** should follow the same format as the Recommendation of Committee A and the Chair/Director.

7. The next page of the packet should be the **"Description of External Evaluators." At least three confidential letters of evaluation are required for inclusion in both tenure and promotion packets *from off-campus scholars or distinguished professionals* in the field who have access to the records or creative work of the candidate.** The purpose of external peer evaluations is to provide an independent, unbiased evaluation of the candidate's scholarly attainment. Someone other than the candidate (usually the Chair and/or Committee A and/or other relevant departmental committee) does the authoritative selection of evaluators and corresponds with evaluators. The Chair/Committee A, or the candidate, may suggest, submit for consideration, or propose potential evaluators. Units should allow, indeed encourage, the candidate to suggest some names. Some appropriate balance should be sought in selection between names suggested by the candidate and suggested by others. **However, at least three of the external evaluators chosen by the unit should have no close academic or personal connections with the candidate: Ph.D. advisers and committee members, coauthors, and close personal friends should not be asked to evaluate the candidate.** In rare cases, such as when a candidate has a very narrow and specialized field of expertise, one or two evaluators with a close professional connection may be included. It is the responsibility of the unit to explain and justify such exceptions to the general requirement.

    The academic unit should describe the method of selection of all evaluators. The unit should also justify the method and the selection of the particular evaluators chosen.

8. Please include copies of the **letters sent to external evaluators** as the next pages of the packet. On the advice of <u>Legal Counsel</u>, the following information should be included in requests for external letters of evaluation:
    "As part of this review process, we are soliciting assessments of Professor_____'s research contributions from academic colleagues and distinguished professionals outside of the University of Oklahoma. These letters of evaluation are treated as confidential by the University to the extent we are permitted to do so by law. These assessments will become part of Professor_____'s tenure dossier to be reviewed in accordance with our

procedures for the tenure decision which generally includes review by the departmental tenure faculty, a select group of college faculty appointed by the dean, the Campus Tenure Committee, and relevant administrators at the University of Oklahoma. We ask for your letter of evaluation and a copy of your own curriculum vita to include with the tenure dossier. In your letter, it is important that you elucidate the extent of your professional or personal relationship with Professor _____; the intent is to identify potential cases of partiality or conflicts of interest that might otherwise not be known by us. We ask that evaluators not provide comments as to whether a candidate should or should not be awarded tenure at the University of Oklahoma but rather comments on how the candidate's research record compares with those who have recently been awarded tenure at your institution."

9. **Copies of all confidential letters of evaluation solicited and received must be included in the dossier.** In no case should fewer than three letters be submitted (usually, five or six letters are included). Academic units are advised to solicit external letters of evaluation early enough that they produce thorough appraisals of the tenure candidates. The Provost's Office recommends that units begin soliciting these during the Spring semester for the coming academic year's tenure cycle. Evaluators should receive an appropriately representative body of work to review and candidates should have input into what pieces of work are sent to evaluators.

In addition to the curriculum vita, a brief but detailed description of the individuals who have provided letters of evaluation for the research, scholarly, or creative activities should also be provided and should include who they are, where they are, what their status in the profession is, whether they were suggested by the Chair/Committee A or by the candidate, why they were selected as reviewers, and whether they have any academic or personal connection with the candidate. (See forms – pages 21 and 22.)

Part II   Candidate Data:

Most of the information will be supplied by the candidate, but the academic unit should assist the candidate by providing certain kinds of data from departmental files. The following information is required for all candidates.

10. **Original letter of appointment (Tenure Candidates Only)**

11. **Annual Progress-toward-tenure evaluation for each probationary year (Tenure Candidates Only)**

12. Summary reports of Annual Faculty Evaluation from date of initial appointment

13. Complete and up-to-date vita including a summary of college and university degrees earned, all professional employment, and all professional honors and awards

14. Teaching Data (provide the following)

    a. Statement of teaching philosophy and activities. Candidates are asked to include a synopsis of both student and peer evaluations of teaching and academic advising, being sure to summarize strong and weak areas at both the undergraduate and graduate levels (including the supervision of master's degree and doctoral thesis

Candidates may contact <u>Laine Stambaugh</u> to view their promotion dossier at any point in the process, unless they have waived access to referee letters.
Check here for <u>IMPORTANT DEADLINES</u>!

2. How the Referee Process Works:

For those of you undergoing promotion review, you are being asked to provide a list of six "indicated" external referees. For purposes of clarification, "external" means that the majority of these referees should be from off-campus, outside the University of Oregon system. If you are a subject specialist, however, you should include your main departmental liaison as one of your "indicated" referees. The Provost's Office appreciates and understands the unique nature and service mission of librarians and library professionals, so you will not be penalized for providing one or two UO names (confirmed by Lorraine Davis on 7/11/02).

Things to Remember:

- "Indicated" Referees are individuals who are known by you, and have agreed to your request to provide positive written letters of recommendation, if asked by the Library Faculty Personnel Committee. These are most likely colleagues and acquaintances you have worked with through participation in professional organizations, publications, and/or other professional activities.
- Be sure to list your "indicated" references in priority order as to whom you would like contacted by the LFPC. Not all may be asked.
- Be sure you include a brief annotation as to why you selected each referee (how you know that person).

The Process:

1. Once Library Human Resources (LHR) receives your list of "indicated" referees, that list is passed on to your immediate supervisor. He/she then adds to that list with a matching number of "non-indicated" referees. "Non-indicated" referees may or may not be known to you or by you, but should be considered experts in the field who are qualified to comment on your individual professional contributions. In the past, these experts have been most gracious and positive about participating in our promotion review process.
2. Your immediate supervisor and/or AUL returns the completed list of "non-indicated" referees to LHR. The two lists are combined into a "Master List," which is then forwarded to the LFPC for consideration. As a committee, they review the list and select those individuals to be contacted for your

case, both from the "indicated" and the "non-indicated" list. One or two "alternate" names will also be selected from the "non-indicated" list, in case any of those decline.

3. LHR assumes you have already asked "indicated" referees if they will write letters, so there should be no surprises!

4. Next, selected "non-indicated" referees are contacted by LHR (via e-mail to speed things up) to see if they are willing to participate. If any respond in the negative, an alternate choice selected by the Committee is contacted.

5. Once LHR receives positive responses from all "non-indicated" referees, a final "Master List" is compiled and placed in your file. You will not be informed ahead of time which referees were selected. If you maintained your right of access to your file, you may view letters after the process is complete.

6. All individuals on the "Master List" are then sent formal letters from the University Librarian, requesting an evaluation of your professional contributions, along with copies of your résumé, personal narrative statement, and any other pertinent documentation (within reason).

ADMINISTRATIVE GUIDELINES FOR HR-23:
PROMOTION AND TENURE PROCEDURES
AND REGULATIONS

(including only section dealing with external letters of assessment)

G.   External Letters of Assessment

1.   External letters of assessment must be obtained for candidates being reviewed for sixth-year or early tenure and for promotion.

2.   Dossiers shall include a minimum of four letters from external evaluators.

3.   The college dean is responsible for obtaining external letters of assessment.

4.   The process of obtaining external letters of assessment should begin far enough in advance of the review process that letters are in the dossier and available to review committees and administrators at all levels of review. If letters arrive after the review process has begun, individuals involved in those levels of review already completed shall be notified by the dean of the receipt of the letters, provided with access to the letters, and provided with an opportunity to reconsider their recommendation.

5.   A log shall be inserted in the dossier to document:

a.   Date of request to external evaluator;

b.   Date of receipt of letter from external evaluator;

c.   Date of entry of letter in dossier.

6.   The log shall not be made available to the candidate at any time.

7.   The college dean shall be responsible for providing a statement explaining the method by which the external evaluators were selected.

8.   The college dean shall be responsible for providing a brief biographical statement about the qualifications of the external evaluator; special attention should be given to documenting the evaluator's standing in his or her discipline as part of the biographical statement.

9. A copy of the letter requesting the external evaluation shall be inserted in the dossier; the request should be for a critical evaluation of the candidate's achievements and reputation within his or her discipline, with reference to the mission and assignment of the candidate. Requests should be for letters of assessment, not for letters of recommendation. (See Appendix C.)

a. If the same letter is sent to all external evaluators, one sample copy of the letter shall be inserted in the dossier. If different letters are used, a copy of each letter shall be inserted in the dossier.

10. Deans are urged to request letters from diverse sources and urged <u>not</u> to request external assessments from the candidate's former teachers and students, those who have collaborated significantly with the candidate or others whose relationship to the candidate might make objective assessments difficult. External evaluators should be asked to describe the nature of their association with the candidate. Evaluators should be in a position to make informed judgments about the candidate=s work.

11. Deans should be consistent in what materials of the candidate they send to external evaluators. Appropriate materials usually include the candidate's vita and, depending on the number involved, all or a representative selection of the candidate's publications. Colleges may if they wish prescribe that candidates' narrative statements be included in the materials sent to external evaluators. Under no circumstance should the dossier as a whole be sent to the external evaluator. Since the focus of evaluation is to be on the candidate's research and/or creative activity, additional items related to teaching or service should not be included in materials that are sent to external reviewers. Units should describe their policy in their promotion and tenure guidelines (or criteria statements).

12. Deans must request external assessments from individuals who are of higher rank than the candidate. It is inappropriate to request assessments from non-tenured assistant professors for candidates for tenure or promotion to associate professor, and so forth.

upon the Director to determine that the candidate meets the 'Specific Qualifications' for Librarian III (see Section V.C., 'Librarian III' below) before referring the matter to the PRC. If the position for which the candidate has applied is substantially different from his or her previous experience (e.g., having a much heavier emphasis on supervisory or management responsibilities), he or she may wish to wait and apply for accelerated consideration once he or she can document success in carrying out all the responsibilities of the position.

If the candidate is to be reviewed for expectation of continuing employment, the full PRC will follow the standard procedures as much as possible for the two-level expectation of continuing employment reviews (described above in Section III.A. above), using the Search Committee's report in place of the Level I Review committee report (the references in the candidate's application shall serve as candidate-supplied names for outside reviewers). The PRC will be required to act quickly and to observe extraordinary confidentiality, as this review process may occur during the employment negotiation process. If necessary, the faculty librarian candidate may be interviewed by the PRC, e.g, to clarify evidence in the candidate's dossier.

The candidate must supply a dossier and names of references to the PRC (and the subcommittee) via the Director's office. The dossier must include information on the candidate's tenure status at his or her current institution (as applicable) and documentation describing the process for granting of tenure at that institution if it has been achieved.

B. Review Materials. The materials used for the faculty librarian's review will consist of the faculty librarian's dossier, the administrative personnel file, and outside review letters.

1. Faculty Librarian's Dossier. The faculty librarian will compile and maintain his or her own personal faculty library dossier to provide documentation in support of his or her reviews. The dossier should contain a current curriculum vitae, a narrative written by the librarian, copies of publications, drafts of works in progress, formal evaluations from students and patrons (as available and appropriate), unsolicited letters, and any other documentation deemed appropriate in supporting his or her review. The narrative must contain a statement of the librarian's outstanding contributions in the areas of job performance, professional development and contributions, and service since appointment to the faculty librarian position within the expectation stream; it should contain sufficient information about the candidate's working philosophy and specific measures of the quality of his or her achievements to assist the review committees in their evaluation of his or her potential as a growing, productive professional. The dossier will be used in both the Level I and Level II reviews, and will be retained in the Director's office until the review is completed, at which time it will be returned to the faculty librarian.

2. Administrative Personnel File. This file is maintained in the Director's office as the administrative permanent employment file. The documentation from this file used for the faculty librarian's review consists of all material related to annual reviews, supervisory letters, and review committee reports as well as any letters or documentation solicited by a review committee. Annual reviews, in addition to evaluating the faculty librarian's performance for the purpose of salary recommendations, should assess the candidate's progress toward meeting the qualifications and criteria for reappointment, promotion, and expectation of continuing employment, as appropriate for the faculty librarian's current rank. For purposes of the review, the candidate's supervisor will write a letter assessing the candidate's record of job performance, professional development and contributions, and service since entering the expectation stream, as well as a summary of mentoring or advice given the candidate about meeting the criteria for promotion or expectation of continuing employment and the candidate's resulting actions. For promotional or reappointment reviews when appropriate, and for all reviews for expectation of continuing employment, the chairperson of the PRC in consultation with the ULS Director will solicit letters from appropriate faculty and librarians, etc., internal or external. Such letters may be solicited by the PRC from relevant non-ULS department chairpersons or school deans regarding the faculty librarian's qualifications for review.

3. Personal Interviews. If necessary, the faculty librarian may be interviewed by either or both of the above committees, e.g., to clarify documentation in the faculty librarian's dossier and/or administrative personnel file. As a general rule, this interview should not be necessary since the faculty librarian dossier and administrative personnel file should provide all the information necessary for committee evaluation.

4. Outside Review Letters. Review letters from outside the university shall be solicited for candidates undergoing review for expectation of continuing employment for ULS Librarian 3 and Librarian 4. In general, letters should be solicited only from faculty librarians at ARL libraries. If circumstances dictate, letters may be solicited from faculty librarians at non-ARL libraries if both the PRC chair and the candidate agree (the candidate would agree in principle, but would not be advised of the names of such individuals except for those reviewers he or she selected). Letters must be solicited from at least six individuals; the candidate, although he or she is not required to submit any names, may submit no more than three of the six names. The reviewer shall be sent the following items: a customized copy of the outside review form letter (Appendix A); a copy of the candidate's Curriculum Vitae; examples of creative activity, i.e., research publications and scholarship; a copy of the ULS Guidelines... with instructions as to which portions therein apply to the current review. The customized outside-review form letter will ask reviewers to provide an assessment of the candidate's professional accomplishments, such as publications, committee memberships, and professional offices held. Reviewers will be asked to evaluate whether the candidate's record of accomplishment is appropriate for the level to which the candidate seeks promotion, as indicated in the ULS *Guidelines'*.

Each letter received must be placed in the candidate's file, and must be accompanied by the following information (in the form of an annotated list of all the letters): name and institution of the reviewer; a summary of the reviewer's credentials; whether the candidate or the review committee provided the reviewer's name; a description of the relationship, if any, between the candidate and the reviewer. The file should identify which individuals, if any, were solicited for reviews but did not provide them, and for what reasons.

In accordance with the University of Pittsburgh Policy #07-06-05, "Access to Employee Personnel Files," University of Pittsburgh Faculty Handbook, July, 2002, letters solicited by a review committee from persons who are not current University of Pittsburgh employees will not be made accessible to the faculty librarian under review.

All of these materials will be used by the full PRC when conducting Level II reviews, with access to the file in the Director's office by appointment. Faculty librarians may review this file according to procedures stated in the University of Pittsburgh policy, #07-06-05.

Return to Top.

The unit director (see Section J) shall provide the candidate with the signed and completed Recommendation Information Form. Within ten (10) days of its receipt, the candidate will sign and return the Form to indicate concurrence with its content, or, if there is a dispute between the candidate and the unit director as to the content of the Form which they are unable to resolve, the candidate shall so indicate in the space provided above his/her signature attaching an explanation to the Form.

The unit director shall attach the candidate's list of documents to the promotion packet. It shall be the responsibility of the unit director to circulate that list and all documents or materials submitted by the candidate, together with any other relevant material to the appropriate reviewing bodies.

The candidate may suggest potential outside evaluators and may discuss with his/her unit director qualified persons from whom letters may be solicited. The candidate, in addition, may prepare a list of persons in his/her field from whom he/she prefers letters of evaluation not be solicited. The candidate shall provide a written explanation for the exclusion of each person on that list. If a letter of evaluation is solicited from an individual on the candidate's not for solicitation list, the candidate's written explanation shall be attached to the individual's letter of recommendation. A unit director or the University Librarian may, at his/her discretion, also attach an explanation for his/her decision to solicit a letter from the individual. Such attachments, whether prepared by the candidate, the unit director or the University Librarian, shall be held, like the letters to which they refer, in confidence.

A candidate who has had time excluded from the probationary period may, upon written request, choose to have University evaluators, evaluative bodies, and outside evaluators informed that his/her record is to be reviewed in the same manner as the record of a faculty member with the normal probationary period.

If the candidate wishes to include a lengthy unpublished manuscript and requires copying services, he/she should contact his or her unit director at least 30 days prior to the date on which copies are needed. The candidate will be charged the prevailing rate for services so provided. If the service cannot be provided, the candidate will be notified promptly.

F.   External Confidential Letters of Evaluation

A minimum of seven external confidential letters of evaluation from qualified persons shall be obtained by the candidate's unit director and/or by the University Librarian. External referees should be selected on the basis of their standing in the field and the institutions with which they are associated. All letters obtained in regard to this candidacy must be included in the promotion packet and forwarded to all levels of review. Preliminary solicitation letters and responses thereto, unsolicited letters and letters from within the University are not included within this category. External letters are not required for reappointment without tenure, but are required for non-tenure track appointments to the senior ranks and for new hires with tenure.

Prior to the solicitation of external letters, the unit director shall submit to the University Librarian a recommended list of referees for each candidate, accompanied by a clear explanation of the suitability of the referee, the relationship of the referee to the candidate and his/her field, and documentation demonstrating the referee's professional standing. The unit director shall make available to the University Librarian any list submitted by the candidate of persons from whom he/she prefers letters not be solicited. Unit directors, in developing lists of appropriate referees to

Page 5

submit to the University Librarian, shall consult the candidate about appropriate experts in his/her field of study, but the selection of external referees must be made by the unit director and University Librarian. After consultation with the candidate and University Librarian, the unit director shall send a preliminary solicitation letter (Appendix G) to individuals he/she has selected to serve as external referees. The preliminary solicitation letter may be sent via e-mail. The text of the preliminary solicitation letter shall not be modified and use of the preliminary solicitation letter is required. The preliminary solicitation letter and the responses thereto do not become part of the promotion packet. It is the unit director's responsibility to keep a copy of the preliminary solicitation letter or e-mails, a list of recipients of the preliminary solicitation letter, dates sent, and responses, confidentially, in the unit until evaluations, grievances, remands, etc. are completed. Under no circumstances shall the candidate contact experts whose names he/she has submitted for consideration, or engage in any substantive discussion about his/her promotion case with any individual whom he/she knows to be serving as an external referee. The presumption is that a unit director and the University Librarian will reach a consensus as to an appropriate list of referees. However, in the event of a disagreement, a unit director is neither obliged to solicit, nor prohibited from soliciting, any particular referee. Similarly, in conducting his/her evaluation of the candidacy as set forth in Section M below, the University Librarian, at his/her discretion, may solicit letters from additional external referees. Such additional letters shall be submitted to evaluative bodies in accord with the procedures set forth in Section H, in which case all letters received after December 1, and until the addition of the University Librarian's letters, shall be submitted.

Sample letters of solicitation are attached in Appendices G-1, G-2 and G-IIL. Letters of solicitation for confidential outside letters of recommendation shall be consistent with the promotion criteria applicable to the candidate. A unit, <u>with the prior approval of the University Librarian and the Executive Vice President for Academic Affairs</u>, may modify the text of the sample letter of solicitation.

No reference which might identify the writers of the confidential letters shall be made in any portions of the promotion materials. Letters will be numbered and may be referred to by their respective number in the narrative statements. Letters of solicitation shall be sent to external referees early enough to permit the referee to complete an appropriately analytical and informative review of the candidate's credentials and to permit reviewing bodies adequate time to consider evaluators' responses.

The original external confidential letters of evaluation, together with a brief explanation of the suitability and professional standing of the referee and the relationship of the referee to the candidate (Form 3-a) and one copy <u>only</u> of the sample letter of solicitation (attached to Form 3), must accompany the original promotion packet forwarded to the University Librarian.[3] Do not include the vitae of referees. All letters received must be submitted for review to <u>all</u> levels of evaluation, except that letters which are received after the December 1 deadline for submission to the Executive Vice President for Academic Affairs will not be considered unless the University Librarian has requested them as additional letters during his/her consideration of the packet.

External confidential letters solicited in a previous year may be used again and included under Form 3. However, selectivity of such letters is <u>not</u> permitted even if the candidacy is later withdrawn pursuant to Section R.; therefore, either all or none of the letters solicited in a previous

---

[3] When a referee relies on a telefaxed letter or an electronic transmission, these may be considered originals in the absence of the original.

Page 6

year must be included, and they must be covered by a copy, supplied by the University Librarian's office, of the earlier Form 3. Preliminary solicitation letters and the responses thereto are not included in this category. If new letters are solicited and if any of the external referees solicited in a prior year are solicited again, then all of the external referees previously solicited (excluding those who declined to evaluate the candidate in response to the preliminary solicitation letter) must be resolicited when the packet being reviewed is the same packet used in a prior evaluation and/or the prior solicitation occurred in either of the two immediately prior years.[4]

In all circumstances, copies of the external confidential letters are to remain in the unit director's office, and the candidate's director shall inform the appropriate tenured members of the unit that such letters are available for review.

G.   Materials to be Used in Review

With the exception of confidential outside letters of recommendation solicited in accordance with these Instructions and those documents that are generally public knowledge such as published student evaluations, published articles, and other similar documents, only those materials in the official personnel file and other materials added to the packet as described in Section H below may be used in conducting the review. The official personnel file for each library faculty member is maintained in the office of the University Librarian.

Documents bearing on the candidate and his/her evaluation which are introduced in the review process are subject to the strictures outlined in the next Section.

H.   Additions to the Packet and the Right to Rebut or Respond

If any document or documents, other than confidential outside letters of recommendation, the official reappointment/promotion forms, continuation pages added to these forms as described in these instructions, reports of reading committees, supplements to confidential letters (Section E, paragraph 4), and materials submitted by the candidate, are added to the promotion packet during the evaluation, a copy of said document(s) shall be transmitted immediately to the candidate; the candidate shall have the right to submit a response or rebuttal within six (6) working days. The re-sponse shall be directed to that level of the evaluation at which the added document was received and shall become a part of the promotion packet. Any documents that are (1) physically present during the evaluation and (2) specifically referred to during the deliberations of the evaluative body and (3) which a majority of the evaluative body agrees have a direct bearing on the evaluation must be added to the packet in accordance with this procedure.

Subsequent to the commencement of the evaluation and prior to final recommendation of the Promotion Review Committee, the unit director shall, upon request of the candidate, add to the packet evidence of a significant change in the status of materials originally submitted by the candidate if: 1) the University Librarian concurs that a significant change has occurred; and 2) such change has occurred since the initiation of the evaluation. If there is a dispute between the candidate and the University Librarian as to whether a significant change has occurred in the status of materials originally submitted by the candidate, the Office of the Executive Vice President for

---

[4] If there is good cause for an exception, it can be made only with the approval of the Executive Vice President for Academic Affairs, upon the recommendation of the University Librarian.

Page 7

THE UNIVERSITY of TENNESSEE / University Libraries

University Links ⬥   A-Z Index / WebMail / Dept. Directory   Enter search t   Library Site Search ⬥ 🔍

Library Support Services

Libraries Home

Library Catalog

Databases

Forms

Help

Services

Branches

Libraries A to Z

AskUs, Now!

Appendix 1
Identifying and Contacting External Reviewers

2004-2005

June 8, 2004

• Start immediately, particularly if you have several candidates up for promotion and tenure. Other than writing the reports, this may be the most difficult part of the whole process.

• Committees of whole chairs are encouraged to meet and work together to identify individuals to contact as potential external reviewers.

• You should find two reviewers from outside the University of Tennessee who are librarians at comparable institutions (where librarians have faculty status or the equivalent). The reviewers should generally work in a similar field, as they will be asked to assess the quality and importance of the candidate's scholarship and contributions to the profession. In the case of promotion, reviewers should be at the rank or above that to which the candidate has applied. In the case of tenure the reviewer must be tenured and at a rank equal to or higher than the candidate. It is acceptable if they know the candidate, but they should not be former teachers, students, or UT faculty. (Manual for Faculty Evaluation).

• There are several strategies to employ to help identify potential external reviewers, including searching academic library websites, searching the literature of the field, and most effective of all, consulting with colleagues for recommendations.

• Send an email inquiry to the individual, following a form similar to the sample below. Be sure to give the individual a (short) deadline for a response to your email, so that you can move on quickly. Telephone contact is also acceptable.

Dear

As part of our promotion and tenure process, the chairs of the faculty review committees at the University of Tennessee Libraries are in the process of identifying librarians at other academic institutions who would be willing to act as external reviewers. We have identified you, as someone who works in a field similar to the candidate and is potentially qualified as an outside reviewer. This email is an initial inquiry to see if you may be willing to serve as an external review for (Jane Doe) who is being reviewed for (*promotion to the rank of Professor*). We would appreciate an immediate reply to let us know if you will be able to work with us.

Ideally external reviewers should hold faculty rank equivalent to that being considered and be tenured at an institution comparable to the University of Tennessee. {*You could add a specific statement here regarding the rank equivalency for each person, i.e. "In order to be a reviewer for Jane Doe you will need to be a tenured full professor or the equivalent."*} Should you consent to serve as a reviewer, you will receive a formal letter of request for an evaluation from our Dean. You will also be provided with a copy of our criteria and selected documents from the candidate's portfolio, including the vita, a narrative statement, and three selections of original work. The Dean will ask that you provide an evaluation of the candidate's professional work and service. She will also ask for your curriculum vita.

We are aware of the time this service requires and we assure you that input from professionals like you is vital to our decision-making process. You should be aware that the State of Tennessee has a Freedom of Information Law. Because of that law, we are unable to guarantee that the candidate will not request to see your letter.

We would appreciate your reply to this email no later than (*select a date and time depending on when you send out the email*). Should you agree to serve as a reviewer, you should receive communication from (*insert name*), Dean of Libraries at the University of Tennessee early in September. (*Date*) has been identified as our deadline for return of evaluations from external reviewers.

Sincerely,

(Your name and rank)

• Be prepared to deal with negative responses or no response at all. If you do not hear back by your deadline then move on and contact the next person on your list. If you are using the telephone to make contacts and end up playing phone tag, then use email. You want to try to get these reviewers lined up as quickly as possible, so that they have plenty of time to receive and read documents, and complete the evaluations.

- Once you have two confirmations for each candidate, send the names and contact information to the Head, LPP or her designate. LPP will send out the letter from the Dean and the necessary documents to the external reviewers.

Table of Contents

HOME

A person in a temporary appointment is not eligible for promotion.

Renewal of appointment applies only to Senior Assistant Librarians as described in Chapter II, Section A.

Associate Librarians who were initially appointed with provisional/non-continuing status may apply for permanent/continuing status as defined in Chapter II, Section B.

The calendar for the promotion, renewal of appointment and permanent/continuing status procedures will be established annually prior to the beginning of Autumn quarter by the Director of University Libraries, within University guidelines and requirements.

Procedures. Prior to the beginning of Autumn quarter, all librarians eligible for promotion or for renewal of appointment, and those Associate Librarians eligible to apply for permanent/continuing status, and their supervisors will be notified by the Administrative Officer Responsible for Personnel. This notification will specify what action is required from the individual and what documentation must be assembled. Not all librarians notified will choose to apply in a given year. While the ultimate responsibility for initiating a promotion request by the dates indicated in this policy rests with each individual, supervisors should encourage qualified librarians to seek promotion at the appropriate time.

In assembling the required documentation, each candidate will be expected to demonstrate that he/she is pursuing a career which enhances the effectiveness and standing of the University of Washington Libraries, supports the mission of the University Libraries, the University and/or learning community, and enhances and contributes to the profession. Complete and accurate documentation is essential to support a request for promotion, permanent/continuing status, or renewal of appointment. Candidates for whom an action is not required may withdraw their request any time prior to the submission of all documentation to the Librarian Personnel Committee.

The candidate must submit 2 copies of the following documentation in three-ring binders to the Administrative Officer Responsible for Personnel in accordance with the calendar established by the Director of University Libraries:

Cover Letter
> A cover letter stating what action is being requested.

References
- The candidate must include the names of at least three references who are knowledgeable about the candidate's professional accomplishments. Individuals in the direct supervisory line should not be included as references. They will be asked to write letters by the Administrative Officer Responsible for Personnel as part of the process.
- For those individuals requesting promotion to the rank of Associate Librarian, or for those individuals holding the rank of Associate Librarian applying for permanent/continuing status at the same rank, there must be at least one reference not employed by the University Libraries who is knowledgeable about the candidate's contributions to the profession.
- For those individuals requesting promotion to the rank of Librarian, there must be at least two references not employed by the University Libraries who are knowledgeable about the candidate's contributions to the profession.

Table of Contents

07/15/04

24

Career Review

A summary document, including a current resume, and other relevant documentation covering the entire professional career. See the Checklist in Appendix E for further details.

Position Descriptions

Copies of position descriptions for all positions held in the University Libraries should be attached. The current position description should be signed by the candidate and his or her direct supervisor. If the position held is less than full-time, the position description should so indicate. If previous position descriptions are not available, a general description of responsibilities for each position should be provided.

The Administrative Officer Responsible for Personnel, in accordance with the calendar established by the Director of University Libraries, will:

Solicit Letters of Reference

Solicit letters of reference from those individuals listed in the candidate's letter. These individuals will be asked to provide specific documentation that the candidate has performed in a manner which:

1. Enhances the effectiveness and standing of the University of Washington Libraries;
2. Demonstrates the candidate's ability to meet the responsibilities of the desired rank;
3. Enhances and contributes to the profession.

Identify an External Reviewer

In addition, for promotions to Associate Librarian or Librarian, or for individuals holding the rank of Associate Librarian without permanent/continuing status who are seeking permanent or continuing status, the Administrative Officer Responsible for Personnel, in consultation with the candidate and supervisors, will identify an individual from outside of the University Libraries to serve as the external reviewer of the file. The external reviewer is chosen for his or her ability to evaluate the candidate's professional accomplishments and activities. The Administrative Officer Responsible for Personnel will send the external reviewer the file which consists of the candidate's letter requesting consideration for promotion, documentation, position descriptions; and the Libraries policies and procedures for promotion; and a copy of the Libraries' mission statement.

A cover letter from the Administrative Officer Responsible for Personnel will include any additional questions to be covered in the external review. The external reviewer will also be asked to provide evaluative comments on whether the candidate has performed in a manner which:

1. Enhances the effectiveness and standing of the University of Washington Libraries;
2. Demonstrates the candidate's ability to meet the responsibilities of the desired rank;
3. Enhances and contributes to the profession.

Solicit Internal Letters

Distribute to University Librarians a list of candidates and their requested action. Librarians who wish to comment on an individual candidate may submit a letter to the Administrative Officer Responsible for Personnel which speaks to the requested action of that candidate as outlined in these guidelines. These internal letters will become part of the candidate's documentation.

07/15/04

Instructions to External Reviewers

September 16, 2002

Dear:

Thank you for agreeing to review the dossier of, candidate for continuing appointment and promotion to the rank of. Enclosed you will find a *curriculum vita*, statement of objectives and copies of publications. Also enclosed is a copy of the *Evaluation of Library Academic Faculty for Promotion and Continuing Appointment* for librarians at the University at Albany to be used for your evaluation. You are asked to base your evaluation on the documentation enclosed. Please address the areas of scholarship and service contributions to the University and the profession, relating them to effectiveness in librarianship as appropriate. Your evaluation should be developed in terms of our guidelines for application for promotion to the rank of *Associate Librarian*.

Your letter should be sent to Meredith A. Butler, Dean and Director of Libraries, University Library 123, University at Albany, State University of New York, 1400 Washington Avenue, Albany, New York, 12222, by.............

The policy of the University Libraries is that all solicited external reviews are confidential. However, the current Agreement between the State of New York and United University Professions requires all solicited evaluators to specify their preference regarding the confidentiality of their responses. In this context, we ask you to return this form or if your response is negative, your assessment will be considered confidential and will not be available to the candidate or the candidate's representative.

We would appreciate it if you would include a copy of your *curriculum vita* with your letter of reference and the confidentiality form. We would appreciate it if you would return the publications.

Again, our thanks for your help in the evaluation of this candidate.

Sincerely,

Geoff Williams, Co-Chair

Deborah LaFond, Co-Chair

APPENDIX D: SAMPLE LETTER TO OUTSIDE EVALUATORS

Dear Referee:

The Department of [*name of department*] is evaluating the academic and professional standing of [*name of candidate*], who is being considered for [*examples: tenure and promotion to associate professor; promotion to full professor*].

Since you are recognized as a leading scholar in [*name of candidate*]'s field, we would appreciate your assistance in assessing his/her record by providing us with a letter of evaluation. We have attached the following materials to help you in evaluating [*name of candidate*]'s record: (1) a curriculum vitae; (2) a summary of his/her workload assignment; (3) a statement in which he/she explains his/her scholarly and professional accomplishments, the goals that have guided them, and his/her future research agenda; (4) copies of University of Arizona departmental and college promotion/tenure criteria; and (5) a representative set of [*examples: articles; slides; tapes*]. If you would like to review additional materials, we would be happy to send them.

In your evaluation, we would appreciate your addressing how well you know the candidate and specific strengths and weaknesses of the candidate's research record, including especially the significance and impact of his/her contributions to the literature and to the field, recognition at national or international levels, and promise of sustained scholarly activity. Please also indicate whether you recommend that candidate be awarded [*examples: tenure and promotion to associate professor; promotion to full professor*] on the basis of your evaluation.

Please note that our criteria for [*promotion; promotion and tenure; tenure*] also include consideration of teaching and service. If you have information and recommendations based on these areas we appreciate your comments related to [*name of candidate*]'s teaching and service.

Your recommendation will be treated with the greatest possible confidentiality permitted by the Arizona Board of Regents' policy and applicable law. I am aware that your consideration and evaluation of the work of our colleague will require considerable time, and I greatly appreciate your willingness to assist us in this way.

We also would appreciate receiving a copy of your abbreviated curriculum vitae. Thank you for participating in this review. Please let me know if you have any questions about the process.

Date

SAMPLE LETTER #1
(for faculty)

Name
Address

Dear Professor _____:

On behalf of the Department of _____ in the College of _____, I
am writing to request your service as an external reviewer for
_____(candidate's name) who has requested consideration for
_____ **(promotion to the rank of associate professor, tenure, promotion to full, etc.)**
Arizona State University, as a major Research institution committed to excellence, is making a
concerted effort to promote and/or tenure the strongest candidates possible in each of its
programs. Accordingly, we would very much appreciate your assistance in evaluating the merits
of Professor _____'s record of research and professional service. Evaluations of the
candidate's instruction are conducted internally, but if you have information about the quality of
Professor _____'s contributions to pedagogy we welcome comments on that aspect of the
candidate's case. **(This should be modified as necessary if the department is sending out
instructional materials for review).**

Enclosed is Professor _____'s vita, copies of (his/her) major publications and papers, **(add
personal statement if you are going to include it)**, and the department/unit promotion & tenure
criteria. Our review procedures require that specialists in the candidate's field evaluate the
candidate's research and professional service record. Neither the names of the referees nor the
contents of their letters are shared with the candidate. Your letter of evaluation will be made
available to the Promotion and Tenure Committee in the Department of _____, and will
become part of the candidate's file reviewed by appropriate committees and administrators at the
college and university levels.

We ask reviewers to do the following –
1. Provide a brief statement regarding your acquaintance with the candidate;

2. Evaluate the candidate's research, creative activity, publications, and professional service
   with respect to their quality and their impact on the candidate's field or subfield -- the
   more detailed your analysis and evaluation of the candidate's work the more useful your
   review will be to our deliberations;

3. Evaluate the suitability of the candidate for tenure **(continuing status if an AP)** and/or
   promotion based upon the enclosed criteria of our department here at ASU;

4. Formulate a comparative judgment regarding the scholarly contributions of the faculty member in relation to other scholars in the field who are at the same point in their careers;

5. Provide a summary recommendation as to whether you support Professor _____'s **promotion & tenure/promotion;**

6. Provide a copy of your curriculum vitae. Your selection as a reviewer of this file is based on the knowledge and appreciation my colleagues and I have for your work in this field. However, institutional consideration of Professor_____'s case inevitably will entail review by people unfamiliar with this field of study and your own work and achievements. To assist those individuals in assessing the information you provide, please include a copy of your vita to familiarize those reviewing this file with your background and accomplishments.

Please return your letter and copy of your current c.v. no later than _____ **(date).** If you have any questions or if you need further information, please feel free to contact me by phone at (480) xxx-xxxx or e-mail: jane.doe@asu.edu.

Thank you very much for taking the time to convey your professional evaluation; I can offer only my gratitude in return.

Sincerely,

_____
Chair/Director

Enclosures

UCI LIBRARIES
LIBRARIAN SERIES
ACADEMIC REVIEW

SAMPLE SOLICITATION OF LETTER OF EVALUATION
FROM OTHER THAN A UCI LIBRARY EMPLOYEE

[Addressee, Address]

Dear :

[X's name, rank, step] is under review in the Librarian series in the Libraries of the University of California, Irvine, for the period from _____ to _____. In the University of California system, letters of evaluation from peers and colleagues are critical to the success of the review of librarians. A letter from you would contribute significantly to this review and would be very much appreciated.

Specifically, I would appreciate your confidential assessment of aspects X's performance about which you have direct knowledge and which are related to one or more of the criteria described in the enclosed *Criteria for Personnel Actions for the Librarian Series.* [*To person suggested by X, when relevant:* X has indicated that you can provide evaluative information on his/her work in _____. If you have directly observed his/her performance in _____ or in any other professional areas, additional evaluative information on this would be appreciated.] [*To person not suggested by X, when relevant:* I am particularly interested in your providing evaluative information on his/her work in _____. If you have directly observed his/her performance in any other professional areas, additional evaluative information on this would be appreciated.] If possible, evaluation of X's performance in comparison with librarians in similar institutions would also be helpful. For your convenience, I am enclosing X's vita.

Please note that I am not asking you to recommend a specific personnel action, but rather to provide me with an **evaluation** of performance of which you have direct knowledge. Your evaluation, together with other factual and evaluative information compiled for the review, will assist me in determining the recommendation for which I am responsible.

[*REQUIRED WORDING*:] Under University of California policy, the identity of authors of letters of evaluation which are included in the personnel review files will be held in confidence. A candidate may, upon request and at certain prescribed stages of the academic personnel review process, be provided access to such letters in redacted form. Redaction is defined as the removal of identifying information (including name, title, institutional affiliation, and relationship to the candidate) contained either at the top of the letterhead or within and below the signature block of the letter of evaluation.

The full text of the body of your letter will therefore be provided to the candidate if so requested. Thus, if you provide any information that tends to identify you in the body of the letter, that information may become available to the candidate. If you wish, you may provide a brief factual

1/01   UCI-LIB-03b

statement regarding your relationship to the candidate at the end of your letter but below the signature block. This brief statement will be subject to redaction and will not be made available to the candidate.

Although we cannot guarantee that at some future time a court or governmental agency will not require the disclosure of the source of confidential evaluations in University of California personnel files, we can assure you that the University will endeavor to protect the identity of authors of letters of evaluation to the fullest extent allowable under the law. [*END OF REQUIRED WORDING*]

I encourage you to be candid and fair in your assessment. Your comments will not only assist me in reaching my recommendation, but will also help me to support X in strengthening his/her performance in the future. I would appreciate having your letter by [date]; if it is not received by then, it may not contribute to my recommendation. If for any reason you cannot write the letter or meet the deadline, please let me know immediately.

Sincerely,

[review initiator's name, title]

Enclosure: X's Vita
    Criteria for Personnel Actions for the Librarian Series

ADMINISTRATIVE CONFIDENTIAL

[insert date]

[insert name]
[insert address]

Dear _____:

[**Susi Smith, Associate Librarian V, of the ____ Library/Department/Unit**] is being considered for [**insert action or actions**] in the Librarian Title series at the UCLA Library. Your name has been provided by the candidate as someone with whom [**he/she**] has interacted in the course of fulfilling [**his/her**] professional responsibilities. In order to develop as complete an assessment file as possible, I invite you to comment on the individual's professional performance, as you are familiar with it. I ask that you focus primarily on the period under review which is from [**Month Year**] to [**Month Year**], but encourage you to also comment as you see fit on any particular achievements and contributions prior to this review period.

The candidate's chief responsibilities as [**insert functional title, i.e., such as Social Sciences Reference Librarian**] include [**insert brief overview of duties**].

In judging suitability for advancement within the Librarian Title series at the University of California, the Committee on Appointment, Promotion & Advancement (CAPA) and the University Librarian consider professional competence and quality of service within the library, professional activity outside the library, University and public service, and research and other creative activities. Professional service and achievement may be judged on the local, state, national, or international recognition it is accorded, on the degree and significance of influence and impact it has had on the University or the profession, and the degree of eminence in creativity, originality, insight, comprehensiveness, and scholarly or professional quality displayed in its execution.

I would appreciate your sending me your objective appraisal of [**insert name of candidate**] activities, accomplishments, and contributions, as you know of them, and your comments relating to professional performance or achievements in areas where you have firsthand knowledge. Of special interest and assistance to those involved in the review process are details that illustrate the contributions this individual has made to the Library, the University, or the profession at large.

Under University of California policy, the identity of authors of letters of evaluation, which are included in the official personnel review files, will be held in confidence. A candidate may, upon request and at certain prescribed states of the academic personnel review process, be provided access to such letters in redacted form. The University of California defines redaction as the removal of identifying information (including name, title, institutional affiliation, and relationship to the candidate) contained either at the top of the letterhead or within and below the signature block of the letter of evaluation. The full text of the body of your letter will therefore be provided to the candidate if so requested. Thus, if you provide any information that tends to identify you in the body of the letter, that information may become available to the candidate. If you wish, you may provide a brief factual statement regarding your relationship to the candidate at the end of your letter but below the signature block. This brief statement will be redacted and will not be made available to the candidate.

Although we cannot guarantee that at some future time a court or governmental agency will not require the disclosure of the source of confidential evaluations in the University of California personnel files, we can assure you that the University will endeavor to protect the identity of authors of letters of evaluation to the fullest extent allowable under the law.

I look forward to hearing from you. Your response by **[insert due date]** will assist in the overall assessment and will be greatly appreciated. If you are not familiar with this individual's activities during the period covered, I would appreciate knowing that.

In mailing your letter, please mark CONFIDENTIAL and mail to my attention at the address below.

Thank you in advance for your cooperation and assistance.

Sincerely,

[insert name]
[insert title]
[insert return address]
[insert e-mail]
[insert phone]

(On Letterhead)

June 7, 2005

XXX
XXX
XXX, XX XXXXX

Dear XX. XXXXXX:

XXXXX is being considered for tenure with promotion to Associate Professor at the Iowa State University Library. Iowa State University requires written evaluation of the candidate's credentials and accomplishments by knowledgeable professionals in librarianship from outside the university/library. Earlier, you agreed to serve in this role, and we are pleased to have your assistance as a reviewer for the candidacy of XXXX. The criteria call for a review of the candidate's practice of librarianship, teaching, research, scholarship, creative activities, and other professional service activities.

Your comments may be directed to the candidate's achievements in the areas listed above or to any others that you deem appropriate, such as the candidate's awareness of current developments in librarianship, or academe generally, continued scholarly growth as exemplified by formal or informal study, participation in institutional affairs and professional organizations, and interest in improving the library profession within the University and society at-large. It would be particularly useful if you could address the *impact* of the candidate's contributions to the field as well as the *quality* of research and publication as compared to others in the field. **Please review the candidate using the Iowa State University Library's *Promotion and Tenure Policies* and not the criteria of your institution or other institutions.**

The review need not take more than a page or two, but should include a recommendation, either positive or negative. Since university officials outside the library will read your letter, please include a brief indication of *your professional credentials* for evaluation of this candidate or a brief vita. Your letter of reference is considered confidential.

We also need to document your personal knowledge of XXXXXX. We would be pleased if you could briefly answer the two questions below as part of your letter to us:

1. Do you know XXXXXX? If yes, please describe your relationship with him (for example, met at a conference, heard presentation at meeting, etc.) If you know him, this should include how long you have known him, whether you have a personal or professional relationship with him, and in general, if there is potential

for conflict of interest. The existence of such relationships per se does not disqualify a person as an external reviewer, but disclosures are necessary.

2. Do you have any association with Iowa State University? If yes, please describe what it is (for example, degrees, served on an external review team, former faculty member, etc.).

The candidate's vita, philosophy statements for research, teaching, and professional practice; his current and previous Position Responsibility Statements; samples of completed research by the candidate published in peer-reviewed journals; and an abridged copy of the Iowa State University Library Promotion and Tenure Policies and Procedures (rev., June 2003) are enclosed.

The Committee would appreciate receiving your letter of reference by **July 29, 2005** or earlier, if possible.

Thank you.

Sincerely,

XXXX xXXXX, Chair
Library Promotion and Tenure Review Committee

Enclosures

LETTER TO EXTERNAL REFERENCES….

Dear_____:

      Professor_____, a member of the faculty of Libraries and Media Services at Kent State University, is standing for __[promotion/tenure]_____ this year. He/she has indicated to me that you have agreed to serve as an external reference for him/her. I am, therefore, requesting that you write a letter in which you address qualifications and achievements relevant to _____ candidacy in each of these categories.

      I am enclosing two documents that you may find helpful. The first is the Libraries and Media Services policy on tenure which outlines our criteria for the achievement of tenure. Candidates at Kent State University are evaluated in the area of job performance, service to the profession, and in the four scholarships defined by Ernest Boyer:

                  The Scholarship of Application,
                  The Scholarship of Teaching,
                  The Scholarship of Integration,
                  The Scholarship of Discovery.

The second document, "The Professional Culture of Libraries and Media Services Faculty at Kent State University," includes our interpretation of Boyer's principles.

      Your comments may be based on both your personal knowledge of Professor _____ work and your perusal of the enclosed materials. Your letters should be sent to me at the address below no later than _____[date]_____. Please contact [_____] if you have any questions.

      Sincerely,

Request for external review of file

DATE

Dear

The Personnel Committee of the University of Louisville Libraries is charged with making recommendations regarding tenure. _____ is now eligible for tenure. (is under review for early tenure.)

The Personnel Committee is preparing to consider her record in order to make a recommendation to the Dean, University Libraries. The University of Louisville requires external review of all research and creative activity for the past five years. We ask that you conduct such a review and write your assessment of the quality of these scholarly products, and the reasons for your assessment.

Please note that in accordance with our guidelines, we ask for your assessment of the work under consideration only, and not for your consideration of Professor _____ or your recommendation regarding her qualifications for tenure.

Enclosed you will find Professor _____'s CV, a copy of the University of Louisville's Minimum Guidelines on External Evaluation and the materials s/he has submitted for review. (The committee is particularly interested in your assessment of _____, but we hope you will assess the other materials as well.) So that we may consider thoroughly your review, we ask that you respond by _____

Thank you very much for your contribution to this process and to academic excellence at the University of Louisville.

Sincerely,

Gail R. Gilbert
Ad Hoc Personnel Committee

3. Personnel Officer's Initial Letter to Potential External Reviewer:

Dear ___ :

At this time of year, the University of Oregon begins the process of considering faculty promotions. I am writing to ask whether you'd be willing to serve as an outside reviewer for _____, _____ Librarian, who is being considered for promotion from Associate Professor to full Professor. The University process requires that the individual has "demonstrated a growing expertise and professional reputation, in the judgment of their professional peers." Would you be willing to serve in this capacity? If you agree, we will send you an electronic copy (let me know if you prefer hard copy) of _____'s dossier along with a copy of our promotion criteria (http://libweb.uoregon.edu/admnpers/promocriteria.html) in the next few weeks, along with a formal letter from our University Librarian. In order to ensure the Library Faculty Personnel Committee has ample time to review all materials, we ask that your evaluative response be sent to us by **November 15.**If you are willing to do this, I will also need either a copy of your resume or a brief biographical description to include with the file--whichever is easier for you to provide. Writing reviews of this nature requires a real commitment of time and attention, so we greatly appreciate your consideration of this request. We ask that you respond to this e-mail by **October 11.** Please let me know if you have any questions!

Thank you

4. Formal Letter Requesting Review Letter

Promotion Letter for _____

Dear _____:

_____, _____ Librarian, _____ Library, is being considered for promotion from Associate Professor to Professor. Such promotions are made only after consulting specialists in the appropriate disciplines, both at the University of Oregon and elsewhere.

Ms. _____ has suggested that you could provide a useful evaluation of her professional achievements and reputation. I shall be grateful if you will write a letter to me, stating your opinion of her scholarship, research accomplishments, publications, and general status within the profession. I have enclosed materials to assist you in this process.

Although Oregon law permits full access of a faculty member to his or her personnel files, Ms. _____has voluntarily waived in advance her legal right of access to the promotion dossier in expectation that this waiver will enable referees to prepare thorough and candid letters. Since this waiver has been reviewed for its legality, I can assure you that your letter will not be seen by the candidate. Your reply to this letter by **November 15, 2005** would be most appreciated in order to comply with the timelines set by the Office of Academic Affairs.

Thank you for your assistance in this important process.

Sincerely,

_____
University Librarian

~~~~~~

Personnel Officer's attached note to referee (above):

I have attached documents that have been submitted regarding Ms. _____'s promotion review. If you would prefer to have me send these in the regular mail, I will be happy to do so. We were just hoping to make the process a bit easier and quicker this way.

You may review the University of Oregon Library Faculty's promotion criteria here: http://libweb.uoregon.edu/admnpers/promocriteria.html.

Ms. _____'s letter explains that we hope to receive your letter by **Nov. 15**, if at all possible. Please do let me know if you have any questions or experience technical problems.

Thank you so much for agreeing to participate in this important process!

PENNSYLVANIA STATE UNIVERSITY

June 16, 2005

[Name and Address of External Evaluator]

Dear [Evaluator]:

Thank you for agreeing to provide a peer evaluation of [Name of Candidate], [Rank and Title of Candidate], who is being considered for final tenure and promotion to the rank of Associate Librarian this academic year. I would very much appreciate your evaluative comments about [Candidate's Name] professional performance.

University policy mandates that I seek evaluations of the candidate from professionals who are qualified to judge the candidate's research, scholarly qualities, career development, and contributions to the discipline. Of particular value would be your appraisal of: (1) [Candidate's Name] research abilities and accomplishments, including papers given at professional meetings; (2) the quality of his/her publications; (3) his/her reputation or standing in the field; (4) his/her potential for further growth and achievement; and (5) whether he/she would be ranked among the most capable and promising librarians in his/her area. It would also be helpful in our deliberations if you could rank [Candidate's Name] contributions in comparison with others you have known at the same stage of professional development. Enclosed you will find a copy of his/her curriculum vita along with copies of publications selected by the candidate. Please also describe the nature of your association with [Candidate's Name].

Responsibilities of Libraries' faculty include combinations of activities such as public or technical service, collection development, instruction, committee assignments, research, and departmental functions. Copies of Penn State's policy on promotion and tenure as well as the University Libraries' criteria are enclosed. Although the criterion "The Scholarship of Librarianship" will be the most important in the evaluation process, we do expect every faculty member to engage in research and scholarly activity appropriate to his or her own area of interest and specialization.

As a final part of this request, I would appreciate it if you would enclose, with your letter of evaluation, a copy of your latest curriculum vita or a brief biographical statement to assist me in writing a brief description of the professional accomplishments of the people who write external letters for the candidates.

I am aware of the imposition that this inquiry provides; however, I assure you that guidance from individuals like yourself is vital to our decision-making process. An early reply would be most appreciated as we do hope to have all letters in the file by August 29, 2005. My office fax number is 814-865-3665 and you may use this method of transmittal for your response with assurances of confidentiality. It is Penn State policy to keep your letter confidential and to share it only with the promotion and tenure review committees and administrators responsible for making recommendations on promotion and tenure.

Thank you for your assistance in this important matter.

Sincerely,

Nancy L. Eaton
Dean, University Libraries

NLE:slw
Enclosures

Date:..Re: Candidate's Name

From: Chair, PRC Review Committee; also include the address, e-mail, and phone/fax numbers to be used by the reviewer in responding to this request, or in seeking further contact before writing the review.

To: Name and address of reviewer

Dear Mr./Ms. ???:

Candidate's name, who is currently a [Librarian II or other rank], is being considered for promotion to the rank of [Librarian III or IV] with expectation of continuing employment. We would very much appreciate your help in evaluating this candidate's professional achievements.

The University Library System expects that those promoted to the rank of [Librarian III, or Librarian IV] will be excellent librarians and mature professionals whose achievements have won recognition (for Librarian IV, exceptional recognition) both by librarians outside the University and by the candidate's faculty-librarian colleagues, and whose presence on the faculty enhances the prestige of the University. Promotion to this rank is not a recognition of length of service, but rather of outstanding librarianship and excellent professional activities. In making your evaluation, which should focus on the achievements of the candidate, it would be helpful if you would:

1. comment upon the degree of recognition achieved in the candidate's field of librarianship;

2. evaluate the scope and significance of the candidate's scholarly achievements and their importance within librarianship or the general discipline;

3. rank the candidate relative to other librarians in the same field of librarianship and at a comparable level of professional development;

4. provide any additional insights that may be helpful in determining whether or not to recommend promotion to [Librarian III, or Librarian IV].

For your convenience we enclose [Candidate's name's] curriculum vitae, copies of some of his/her latest works (see Guidelines…, appropriate sections for ULS descriptions of publications and creative works), and a copy of the ULS *Guidelines*....

It is the policy of the University of Pittsburgh that external letters be held in confidence. However, in the event of litigation or a governmental investigation, the candidate or others may gain access to the information contained in these letters.

We would appreciate receiving your evaluation by [Month Date, Year] if possible, since the review process requires all materials to be in hand as early in the academic year as possible. We are very grateful for your help in this matter.

Sincerely,

Signed, Name and Title

(DATE)

(ADDRESS)

Dear Professor:

(CANDIDATE) is being considered for promotion to (POSITION). Your name has been suggested to the Purdue University Libraries Primary Promotions and Tenure Committee as someone who could write a recommendation on (CANDIDATE)'s behalf. Candidates for promotion are evaluated on quality of performance in these areas:

- Demonstrated excellence in the field of librarianship
- Excellence in research, scholarship, and/or creative endeavor
- Excellence in continuation and/or service

The Promotion and Tenure Committee would like for you to provide an assessment of (CANDIDATE)'s performance for those areas about which you have direct knowledge. Please also add a brief description of your relationship with the candidate.

I am enclosing the following documents to assist you in understanding our expectations and in providing our assessment:

- "Promotions and Tenure Policy for the Libraries,"
- Resume for (CANDIDATE) identifying highlights,
- Selection of (CANDIDATE)'s publications.

Under our University policies, your letter will be held in confidence to the extent permitted by law. Under certain circumstances a promotion or tenure file may be mandated by a federal or state agency whose responsibility it is to investigate an allegation of discrimination involving promotion or tenure. In our opinion, the likelihood of this eventuality is remote and we would, under no circumstances, divulge such information without a lawfully issued (subpoena) demand for the information. Purdue would also vigorously resist any efforts to gain access to your letter under Indiana Public Records law.

Though your letter is confidential, information from it or a summary of it may be included in the written review of the Libraries Primary Promotions and Tenure Committee. Your letter will also accompany the promotion document. On behalf of the Committee, I would appreciate your making every effort to return your comments to me by DATE. Please send the letter to:

(NAME of CHAIR of P&T COMMITTEE)
Purdue University Libraries ADMN
504 West State Street
West Lafayette, IN 47907-2058

If for any reason you can not send a written statement by this date, or if you have any questions, please contact me at PHONE NO. or E-MAIL. Your assistance is greatly appreciated.

Sincerely,

Prof. xxxxx xxxxx, Chair
Purdue Libraries Primary Promotions
& Tenure Committee

APPENDIX G

SAMPLE LETTER – PRELIMINARY SOLICITATION OF SERVICE AS EXTERNAL
CONFIDENTIAL REFEREE
(may be sent via e-mail)

Dear (name):

We are reviewing the dossier of (name), currently (tenured/untenured, rank) at Rutgers
University for potential promotion to the rank of (tenured/untenured, rank). I am contacting
you in my role as unit director to ask if you would be willing to review Professor (name)'s
scholarly materials and provide us with a substantive and rigorous evaluation of (his/her)
work.

If you agree to help, we will send you the official request, Professor (name)'s cv and
samples of (his/her) research. We would need to receive your evaluation by (date), and we
ask that you consider the specific questions in the cover letter as well as all of the materials
that we will send you.

At this time we ask that you respond no later than (date), only to indicate whether or not
you are able to participate in the evaluation. In fairness to the process, any substantive
comments to be presented to our committees of evaluation must be based on a reading of the
full packet of materials mentioned above.

Your evaluation letter will be maintained in confidence as stipulated by University
policy, and it is important to the integrity of our process that this request be kept
confidential.

Thank you very much for considering this request.

Sincerely,

(Unit Director)

APPENDIX G-1

SAMPLE LETTER – SOLICITATION OF EXTERNAL CONFIDENTIAL
EVALUATION FOR INDIVIDUALS WHO ARE CANDIDATES FOR PROMOTION TO
LIBRARIAN II

Dear (name):

The (library unit) is considering the promotion of untenured (current rank and name) to
Librarian II with tenure effective July 1, 20__.

To assist the Library and the University in this consideration, it is the University's
practice to solicit written evaluations from experts outside the University. These letters are
essential in assisting us to evaluate (name)'s scholarly achievements in librarianship and
(his/her) professional standing in comparison with colleagues in (his/her) field. It is not
necessary that you be personally familiar with (name)'s work or professional contributions.
We request that you draw upon your knowledge of the field and the documentation provided
to evaluate (name).

I am writing to ask if you would send me a confidential letter assessing (name)'s
scholarship and librarianship. We would especially like your evaluation of the originality
and quality of (his/her) achievements, their impact upon the field, and the value of (his/her)
contributions to the profession. We would also appreciate your assessment of (name)'s
accomplishments relative to others in comparable positions in the profession nationally and
internationally, as well as your judgment of whether (his/her) work meets the requirement
for someone being considered for promotion at your institution. In addition, if you are able
to comment upon (name)'s service to the profession, we would appreciate receiving your
assessment in that area.

We would also appreciate it if you would provide us with a short biosketch, including a
brief description of your areas of expertise and current research interests, and/or curriculum
vitae. Finally, please advise us of your relationship to the candidate, if any, and the prior
basis of your knowledge of the candidate's work, if any.

For your information, I am enclosing a copy of (name)'s curriculum vitae and selected
publications. If you would like to have copies of any of the publications beyond those
which I have enclosed, I will be happy to send them to you. I have also included a copy of
the applicable criteria for librarianship and scholarship to inform your assessment. I would
appreciate your response by no later than (date). If you are unable to respond by then,
please let me know.

I want to assure you that the University will make every effort to maintain the
confidentiality of the letter you write. Let me express in advance our deep appreciation for
your assistance in this matter.

Sincerely,

(Unit Director)

Enc.

Dear_____:

_____ is a candidate for_____ at The University of Tennessee, Knoxville and has submitted your name as an evaluator of _____ professional accomplishments.

In your evaluation, please be as specific as possible.

    1) Describe your professional relationship with the candidate.

    Please comment on _____'s performance as a librarian, being as specific as possible about what you know of the kind and value of the candidate's work in the discipline (research, scholarship, professional development) and contributions to the profession.

    2) Describe and evaluate professional work and service to the libraries, the university, or the public made by the candidate. I have enclosed copies of our criteria for _____ and _____'s curriculum vitae. In addition the candidate has selected the enclosed documents reflecting their creative and scholarly output for your review.

The university emphasizes the importance of selecting referees who are at rank for which the candidate is being considered or higher and requires a summary statement about each referee. Therefore, I would appreciate a copy of your curriculum vitae, and an indication, when appropriate, of your faculty rank or the equivalent in your organization. We are aware of the time this request requires; however, we assure you that guidance from scholars ("professionals" when writing to librarians) like you is vital to our decision-making process.

You should be aware that the State of Tennessee has a Freedom of Information Law. Because of that law, we are unable to guarantee that the candidate will not request to see your letter.

Please send your evaluation to Barbara I. Dewey, Dean of Libraries, John C. Hodges Library, The University of Tennessee, Knoxville, TN 37996-1000 by October 15, 2004. If you prefer, you may use e-mail for your response (bdewey@utk.edu).

Thank you for your cooperation in this important process. We deeply appreciate your assistance.

Sincerely,

Barbara I. Dewey
Dean of Libraries

Enclosure
Revised 2004.

BACK NEXT
HOME

Dear _____ :

_____ is a candidate for _____ at The University of Tennessee, Knoxville. The chair of the Committee of the Whole has identified you as a potential external evaluator because of your expertise in areas associated with their work. The University of Tennessee's promotion and tenure process requires that we seek evaluations from persons who have not worked with the candidate and, thus, _____ is not aware of our request.

We would appreciate your frank appraisal of the candidate's professional work and creative achievements, the quality of publications or other creative work, reputation or standing in the field, and potential for further growth and achievement. We have included a curriculum vitae and a sample of pertinent publications selected by the candidate for your review. Please also describe your professional relationship and/or knowledge of the candidate. Also enclosed are criteria for _____.

The university emphasizes the importance of selecting referees who are at rank for which the candidate is being considered or higher and requires a summary statement about each referee. Therefore, I would appreciate a copy of your curriculum vitae, and an indication, when appropriate, of your faculty rank. We are aware of the time that our request requires; however, we assure you that guidance from scholars ("professionals" when writing to librarians) like you is vital to our decision-making process.

You should be aware that the State of Tennessee has a Freedom of Information Law. Because of that law, we are unable to guarantee that the candidate will not request to see your letter.

Please send your evaluation to Barbara I Dewey, Dean of Libraries, John C. Hodges Library, The University of Tennessee, Knoxville, Tennessee 37996-1000 by October 15, 2004. If you prefer, you may use e-mail for your response (bdewey@utk.edu).

Thank you for your cooperation in this important process.

Sincerely,

Barbara I.Dewey
Dean of Libraries

Enclosure
Revised 2004.

UNIVERSITY OF WASHINGTON

UNIVERSITY LIBRARIES
Office of the Dean

February 21, 2006

Ms. Jane Smith
Head, Any Department
Any Library
Any Town, Any State 00000

Dear Ms. Smith:

Thank you very much for your willingness to assist the University of Washington
Libraries. Your evaluative comments on John Doe, Librarian, will be an important
component of John's documentation as he seeks promotion to the rank of Associate
Librarian with permanent status.

John currently holds an appointment as a Senior Assistant Librarian with provisional
status in the University of Washington Libraries. The documentation John submitted in
support of his request for promotion is enclosed for your consultation.

Your evaluation of John's professional accomplishments and activities will become part
of the documentation reviewed by the supervisory line and by the ad hoc Peer Committee
and Librarian Personnel Committee, and it will not be made available to the candidate.

We ask that you provide evaluative comments on whether John has performed in a
manner which:

> Enhances the effectiveness and standing of the University of Washington Libraries;
> Demonstrates his ability to meet the responsibilities of the desired rank; and,
> Enhances and contributes to the profession.

For your information, I am enclosing the University of Washington Libraries' Mission
Statement and, from the Librarian Personnel Code, the 1) Introduction, 2) the Chapter on
Rank and Status, 3) the Guidelines for Appointment, Renewal of Appointment and
Promotion, and, 4) the Guidelines for Activities Supporting Reappointment, Promotion,
and Permanent/Continuing Appointment.

482 Allen Library   Box 352900   Seattle, Washington 98195-2900
Phone: 206.543.1760   Fax: 206.685.8727   www.lib.washington.edu

Page 2
Jane Smith

Please let me know if you have any questions or if I can assist you in any way. I can be reached at 206-685-1978 or by e-mail at cecuwa@u.washington.edu. If at all possible, please respond by Friday, January 13, 2006. Your evaluation and the candidate's documentation are to be returned to me at this address:

First Class Mail	UPS / FedEx
Charles E. Chamberlin Deputy Director of Libraries 482 Allen Library Box 352900 University of Washington Seattle, Washington 98195-2900	Charles E. Chamberlin Deputy Director of Libraries 85 Allen Library Loading Dock University of Washington Seattle, Washington 98195-2900

Please return the evaluation and documentation by either first class mail or UPS/FedEx. If you personally pay for the postage, please send me an email noting the mailing costs so I may reimburse you.

We are deeply appreciative of your assistance.

Charles E. Chamberlin
Deputy Director of Libraries

CEC:sb
Enclosures

Librarians\Appointment-Reappointment\ExternalReviewers\ExternalReviewerRefReq2005.doc

SELECTED RESOURCES

DOCUMENTS

Books and Journal Articles

Bradigan, Pamela S., and Carol A. Mularski. "Evaluation of Academic Librarians' Publications for Tenure and Initial Promotion." *Journal of Academic Librarianship* 22, no. 5 (September 1996): 360–65.

Hook, Sara Anne, N. Doug Lees, and Gerald Powers. *Post-Tenure Review.* SPEC Kit 261. Washington, DC: Association of Research Libraries, October 2000.

Kyrillidou, Martha, and Mark Young. *ARL Annual Salary Survey 2005–2006.* Washington, DC: Association of Research Libraries, 2006.

Leysen, Joan M., and William K. Black. "Peer Review in Carnegie Research Libraries." *College & Research Libraries* 59, no. 6 (November 1998): 512–22.

Poston, Lawrence. "Neither Bane nor Boon: External Reviewing in the Tenure and Promotion Process." *ADE Bulletin* 77 (Spring 1984): 44–46.

Reilly, Lyn, Joan Carlisle, Kathleen Mikan, and Melissa Goldsmith. "External Review for Promotion and Tenure in Schools of Nursing." *Nurse Education Today* 16, no. 5 (October 1996): 368–72.

Schlozman, Kay Lehman. "External Reviews in Tenure and Promotions Decisions: How Does the Process Work? How Should It?" *Political Science & Politics* 31, no. 3 (1998): 623.

Schwartz, B.N., and R.G. Schroeder. "External Reviews: What Is Being Done?" *Journal of Accounting Education* 15, no. 4 (Autumn 1997): 531–47.

Promotion and Tenure Documents on the Web

University of Arizona. Vice Provost for Academic Affairs. Continuing Status & Promotion Process.
http://web.arizona.edu/~vprovacf/c&p/

Auburn University. Faculty Handbook. 3. Faculty Personnel Policies and Procedures. 11. Procedure for Promotion and Tenure.
http://www.auburn.edu/academic/provost/handbook.html

University of Kentucky. Promotion and Tenure Contract Renewal. A guide for University of Kentucky Librarians.
http://www.uky.edu/Libraries/ptguide.doc

University of Maryland. Documents for the Faculty Promotion and Permanent Status Review Process.
http://www.lib.umd.edu/groups/lfa/pps_process_docs.html

University of Oregon. Library Faculty Evaluation Procedures & Criteria for (Ranked) Officers of Administration.
http://libweb.uoregon.edu/admnpers/faceval.html

Yale University. Library Human Resources. Promotion Review.
http://www.library.yale.edu/lhr/pp/promotion.html

Note: All URLs accessed August 2, 2006.

S P E C K I T T I T L E L I S T

SPEC KIT PRICE INFORMATION

Individual Kits: $35 ARL members/$45 nonmembers, plus shipping and handling.

Individual issues of the Transforming Libraries (TL) subseries: $28, plus shipping and handling.

SHIPPING & HANDLING

U.S.: UPS Ground delivery, $10 per publication.

Canada: UPS Ground delivery, $15 per publication

International and rush orders: Call or e-mail for quote.

PAYMENT INFORMATION

Make check or money order payable in U.S. funds to the ASSOCIATION OF RESEARCH LIBRARIES, Federal ID #52-0784198-N. MasterCard and Visa accepted.

SEND ORDERS TO: ARL Publications Distribution Center, P.O. Box 531, Annapolis Junction, MD 20701-0531
phone (301) 362-8196; fax (301) 206-9789; e-mail pubs@arl.org

ORDER ONLINE AT: http://www.arl.org/pubscat/index.html